THE DEEPEST ACCEPTANCE
Radical Awakening in Ordinary Life

JEFF

THE DEEPEST ACCEPTANCE
Radical Awakening in Ordinary Life

FOSTER

souNDs TRue
Boulder, Colorado

Sounds True, Inc.
Boulder, CO 80306

SOUNDS TRUE is a trademark of Sounds True, Inc.

Published 2012

Cover and book design by Rachael Murray
Cover image © EpicStockMedia, Shutterstock.com

Excerpt from "My Brilliant Image" by Hafiz, from the Penguin publication *I Heard God Laughing, Poems of Hope and Joy,* copyright © 1996 & 2006 Daniel Ladinsky, and used with his permission.

Printed in Canada

Library of Congress Cataloging-in-Publication Data

Foster, Jeff.

The deepest acceptance : radical awakening in ordinary life / Jeff Foster.

    p. cm.

ISBN 978-1-60407-855-8

1. Spiritual life. 2. Self-acceptance--Religious aspects. 3. Self-perception--Religious aspects. I. Title.

BL624.F663 2012

204'.4--dc23

                              2012016001

Ebook ISBN 978-1-60407-914-2

10 9 8 7 6 5 4 3 2 1

I wish I could show you
When you are lonely or in darkness
The Astonishing Light
Of your own Being.

HAFIZ, from "My Brilliant Image"

Contents

Acknowledgements

With love and deep gratitude to:
  Amy Rost
  Tami Simon
  Matt Licata
  Julian and Catherine Noyce of Non-Duality Press (UK)
  Menno van der Meer and Jeannine de Klerk
  Sherie Davis and Amy O'Neil
  Lynda and Sid Foster
  Maurizio and Zaya Benazzo
  Mike Larcombe, Nic Higham, and Scott Kiloby
  Arlene Eastland

. . . and all the other wonderful beings I've met on this incredible journey.

Author's Note

It seems to me that all our problems, all our suffering and conflicts, both personal and global, stem from one basic problem: our ignorance of who we really are. We have forgotten our inseparability from life, and so we have started to fear it, and out of that fear we have gone to war with it in various ways. We have gone to war with our thoughts, our feelings, our emotions, our bodies, with the present moment itself. In our efforts to protect ourselves from pain, from fear, from sadness, from discomfort, from failure, from the parts of life we have been conditioned to believe are bad or negative or dark or dangerous, we have stopped being truly alive.

The armor we wear to protect ourselves from a full experience of life is called the separate self. But our armor does not really protect us—it just keeps us comfortably numb.

Spiritual awakening—realizing that you are not who you think you are—is the answer to this basic problem of humanity. These days there are many books available on this topic, and it seems that more people than ever are discovering ancient teachings that used to only be available to a select few. But there is a trap here. Spirituality can easily become just another layer in our armor. Rather than facilitating our opening up to life, it can shut us off even more. Spiritual concepts and clichés like "There is no self" or "This is not my body" or "Duality is just an illusion" can simply be new beliefs to cling to, new ways of avoiding life and pushing the world away, which result in more suffering, for us and for those we love.

The spiritual awakening I talk about in this book is not about protecting yourself more; it's about realizing that who you really are does not need protection, that who you really are is so open and free and loving and deeply accepting that it allows all of life into itself. Life cannot hurt you, because you *are* life. So the present moment is not an enemy to be feared, but a dear friend to be embraced. Yes, true spirituality does not strengthen your armor against life—it destroys it.

Spiritual awakening is actually very simple. It is the timeless recognition of who you really are, the consciousness prior to form. But actually *living* that recognition in day-to-day life, not forgetting or losing it or letting it go to your head— that's where the real adventure of life begins. And that's where many people seem to struggle—spiritual seekers and spiritual teachers alike.

It's one thing to know *who you really are* when life is easy and things are going well for you. It's another thing to remember this in the heat of the moment, when things fall apart, when life gets messy and your dreams turn to dust. In the midst of physical and emotional pain, addictions, relationship conflicts, and worldly and spiritual failure, often we can feel less awakened and more separate from life, from each other, and from who we really are, than ever. Our happy dreams of our enlightenment can quickly evaporate, and acceptance can seem a million miles away.

We can see the messiness and beauty of day-to-day human existence as something to be avoided, transcended, or even obliterated, *or* we can see it for what it really is: a secret and constant invitation to wake up *now*, even if we believe we already woke up yesterday. Life, in its infinite compassion, won't let us rest on our laurels.

If my earlier books were *descriptions* of spiritual awakening, this book addresses far more important questions: *How* can that awakening be lived day-to-day? *How* can we accept the present moment even when the present moment seems totally unacceptable to us? Is "*How* can we accept the present moment?" even the right question? Are we actually *separate* from the present moment in the first place?

I teach one thing and one thing only: *a deep and fearless acceptance of whatever comes your way.* This is not passive surrender or cold detachment, but an intelligent and creative emergence into the mystery of the moment. This book comes after many years of listening and speaking to thousands of people on the spiritual path—hearing their concerns, answering their challenging questions, meeting them in their pain and grief and daily struggles and fears, and gently pointing them not to a future enlightenment, but to a deep and unconditional acceptance within their present-moment experience, the deep acceptance that they are in their essence.

Welcome to ordinary life, dear explorer—the final frontier of spiritual awakening. May you boldly go where no one has gone before!

With love from yourself,
Jeff Foster

Part I

AWAKENING TO DEEP ACCEPTANCE

The Wholeness of Life

*The real voyage of discovery consists not in seeking
new landscapes, but in having new eyes.*
MARCEL PROUST

The wrinkles on your elderly father's hands. The cry of a
newborn baby. A sculpture in an art gallery. A certain combi-
nation of notes in a piece of music. A dewdrop on a blade of
grass. A momentary look on a stranger's face, suddenly and
unexpectedly melting your heart. Wholeness suddenly pierc-
ing through separation.

Life is rich with mystery.

I was recently talking to a friend of mine who had just
given birth. My friend is a scientist, a "rational thinker," and
an atheist, with no interest in spirituality or religion or anything that cannot be proved through "peer-reviewed research,"
as she calls it. She believes that life is all about working hard,
providing for your family, saving for old age, and eventually
retiring and enjoying "the good life" before you die.

And yet, as she talked about her experience of her daughter's birth, her words were not those of an atheist; they were
religious words, spiritual words, words pregnant with awe and
wonder and the overwhelming miracle of creation. She talked

about the miracle of life itself—the mystery of birth and of death, the cosmic riddle that permeates all things. She told me that as she held her newborn daughter for the first time, all self-centered thoughts fell away, past and future dissolved, and suddenly there was only this—only life itself, present, alive, mysterious. There was only this precious moment, here and now, and nothing more.

She told me how she wept with gratitude upon seeing her daughter's tiny little fingers for the first time—how delicate they were, how fragile. She told me how amazed she was that something so mysterious and *alive* could have emerged from her, how something could have come out of nothing, how life could produce life out of itself, how the same life that was present at the Big Bang is somehow also here, in the form of this tiny, pink creature. She was suddenly consumed with an unconditional love—for her daughter, for all babies and mothers everywhere, for all existence. It was a love she had no words for. All peer-reviewed research crumbled in the face of the incomprehensible vastness of present-moment experience.

My friend, the scientist, the rational thinker, the skeptic, had temporarily become a nondual mystic, and she didn't even know it. For a moment, she had touched the wholeness of life, the wordless mystery that permeates all creation. For a moment, she had *fallen in love* with existence; the separation between her and life had fallen away, to reveal a love with no name.

I have met many people over the years who have become interested in spirituality because of certain strange, inexplicable, incomprehensible experiences or realizations they'd had, often out of the blue—experiences that were later hard to put into words and harder still to communicate to their friends and families.

Artists talk about the self falling away when they are absorbed in painting. Musicians tell of how, while absorbed in their music, there is *only* the music, and they, as a separate entity, vanish into it, as if they've been absorbed by life. They are not playing the music—they *are* the music, playing itself. Athletes talk about getting into the flow or entering the zone, a place where running or riding or jumping happens effortlessly, and the body functions perfectly even though they no longer experience the body as their own. Actors talk about disappearing into their characters, about losing themselves in a role, about how when they are really acting, there's nobody there acting. When they are later congratulated on their performance and asked how they managed to achieve it, they have to admit that they *really don't know.*

Or you're walking through the park, and suddenly there's no *you* walking—there is only the wind on your face, the rustle of leaves, the laughing of children, and the barking of dogs. You disappear, and you become everything—or everything disappears, and you become nothing. Words simply don't do it justice.

Sometimes the stories are less dramatic. You're washing the dishes, and suddenly the glistening soap bubbles become the most fascinating things in the universe—indeed, the soap bubbles *become* the universe in that moment. And all your problems, your fears, your anxieties, your desperate search for a better life, for fame, for glory, for love, for enlightenment, fade away. Everything is deeply okay again—cosmically okay. Even though your life situation hasn't changed—there are still bills to pay, children to feed, work to do, pain to feel—your relationship to it all has suddenly transformed. In an instant, you're no longer a separate individual struggling to find wholeness. There is *only* wholeness. You're back in the womb of life—a womb you never really left. And yet, ordinary life is still present, and you continue to function in the world effortlessly.

Science has a hard time explaining these experiences—or nonexperiences or whatever you want to call them—for they take us beyond the world of cause and effect, subject and object, observer and observed, absolute and relative, inside and outside, even time and space. They are hard to prove or demonstrate logically, scientifically, philosophically. But to those who experience them, they are more real than anything. Call them awakenings or peak experiences or simply raw encounters with life as it is. It doesn't really matter what you call them, because in the end, the words always come later.

Existence is rich with mystery and wonder, and sometimes, without warning, light can shine through the cracks in the separate self. For a few brief moments, there is the cosmic suggestion that life is somehow infinitely *more* than what it appears to be. The most ordinary of things can easily turn extraordinary, making us wonder if, perhaps, the extraordinary is hidden *in* the ordinary always, just waiting to be discovered.

Yes, perhaps the ordinary things of life—broken old chairs, bicycle tires, sunlight reflecting on broken glass, a smile from a loved one, the cry of a newborn baby—are actually not ordinary at all. Perhaps hidden in their ordinariness is something extraordinary. Perhaps all of those things we take for granted are actually divine, sacred, infinitely precious expressions of a wholeness, a Oneness that cannot be expressed in thought or language.

And perhaps this wholeness is not "out there," somewhere else or in the future, waiting to be uncovered. Perhaps we don't need to go to the farthest reaches of the universe to find it. Perhaps it is not in the heavens or hidden away in the deepest depths of our souls. Perhaps wholeness is right here, where we already are—in *this* world, in *this* life—and perhaps we have somehow blinded ourselves to it in our obsession with our search for it.

Modern physics is now confirming what spiritual teachings throughout the ages have always been pointing to: everything is interconnected, and nothing exists separately from anything else. We have invented many words over the years to try to point to this cosmic wholeness, words like *spirit, nature, Oneness, Advaita, nonduality, consciousness, awareness, aliveness, Being, Source, Existence, Isness, Tao, Buddha Mind,* and *presence.* We could sit and argue for a hundred years about what the wholeness of life actually *is,* but I wonder if we'd end up arguing over words and miss what the words are pointing to. So pick your favorite word for wholeness, because in the end it's not about the words. You call it the *Tao*. I call it *Life*. She calls it God. He calls it consciousness. Someone else calls it *nothing*, and someone else calls it *everything*. Someone else likes to keep silent about it. An artist paints pictures about it. A musician writes music about it. A physicist tries to touch it through complex calculations and mind-bending theories. A poet or philosopher juggles with words to try to reach it. A shaman gives you strange substances so you may see it for yourself. A spiritual teacher points you to it both with language and silence.

The point is, whatever *it* is will never ultimately be put into words. Thoughts and words fragment wholeness; they break up a unified reality into separate things: bodies, chairs, tables, trees, the sun, the sky, me, you. The world of thought is the world of duality, the world of *things*.

Of course, I'll be using a lot of words in this book. Words are very useful for writing and reading books! But the most important thing to remember is that *it's not about the words*. It's about the wholeness of life itself—and that comes before *all* words, even the word *wholeness*.

There is a great silence and rest that permeates all of these words, and it is this inner stillness that I speak from. This entire book is a love letter from stillness to itself—from who I really am, to who you really are.

I used to volunteer in a hospice, and I spent time with people who were in the final weeks or days or even hours of their lives. Often the patients would confess to me that it was only at that moment, as the curtain was about to fall, that they were really opening their eyes to the performance. Only then were they starting to see how precious life is—and always had been. Many of them talked about their regrets. Regrets over not having lived life to the fullest. Regrets over not having loved enough, over having held their feelings back out of fear of rejection. Regrets over not having been more honest and open in their relationships. Regrets over working themselves until they were sick, in pursuit of a future that never came and was never going to come. If only they'd known that life had other plans in store for them, they might have opened their eyes sooner.

For some of them, it was only when *time* had been stripped away from them that they were really starting to explore life. They didn't have time to live in hopes and dreams anymore— they only had time to live. Some had taken up art; some were learning to play an instrument or sing or dance for the first time. One woman I met had finally found the courage to record her debut album. For her whole life she had hidden away, singing in the shower when she was alone, protecting herself from ridicule and rejection. But now in the last weeks of her life, when she had nothing to lose, she was singing her heart out, as if nobody were listening, as if she had already died and there was no longer anything to fear. Ridicule and rejection were no longer her enemies.

One day, I was playing chess with a female patient. We barely spoke to each other as we played. Her head was shaved, and she was obviously weak from months of chemotherapy. But she was so *present* with me for that hour or so that we were together. She was so in the here and now, so absorbed by life, so *fascinated by everything,* like a newborn baby. "Checkmate," she said with a smile, as she cornered my king. She died that evening, but during that game she was more alive, more open to experience, more in love with the present moment, than many people who have another fifty years to live. Being present has nothing to do with time.

Why does it often take extreme life situations to bring back an awareness of the magic and mystery of life? Why do we often wait until we're about to die before discovering a deep gratitude for life as it is? Why do we exhaust ourselves seeking love, acceptance, fame, success, or spiritual enlightenment in the future? Why do we work or meditate ourselves into the grave? Why do we postpone life? Why do we hold back from it? What are we looking for exactly? What are we waiting for? What are we afraid of?

Will the life we long for really come in the future? Or is it always closer than that?

This book is about the wholeness of life and about the possibility of discovering that wholeness *right now*—not next year, not tomorrow, not "one day," but right now, *in the midst of present experience,* in the midst of whatever is happening, even if what's happening is discomfort and pain and a longing to be free.

This book is about finding out who you really are, beyond who you think you are, beyond who you've been taught you are, beyond your story about who you are, beyond all your concepts and images of who you are. And it's about discovering the ways in which, in forgetting who we are, in our attempts to build and hold up what basically amounts to a false, thought-constructed image of ourselves, we go to war with present experience, with each other, with the planet. Our inner conflict becomes outer conflict. When I am at war within myself, I go to war with you. What I reject in myself, I reject in the world. And that rejection leads to suffering of every kind. We addict ourselves to substances or habits, even seemingly good ones, to avoid what we don't like about ourselves. We battle with painful emotions. We search for another person and a relationship that will complete us. We desperately seek to escape discomfort by becoming enlightened.

In this book, I'll hold up a magnifying glass to the place where conflict begins in us, because the place where conflict begins in us is also the place it can end.

It is estimated that in the twentieth century alone, human beings managed to kill more than 200 million other human beings in wars and through genocide. Human beings seem to be unique among the planet's organisms in that we harm and kill other humans not just to protect ourselves physically, not just in pursuit of food and territory, but also in defense of *images*. We kill in the name of every kind of image—ideologies, philosophies, belief systems, spiritual paths, worldviews. We kill in our attempts to create our image of heaven upon the earth, to impose our image of the world upon other human beings who are not like us. We kill in the name of images of reality, images of truth and falsehood, images of who we are and who others are in relation to us—images that rarely, if ever, correspond to reality. Where can this violence end?

It is fashionable these days to talk about a shift in human consciousness that is happening on the planet—the idea that human beings are in the process of reaching some higher state of consciousness. But instead, I think what we're really doing is developing a new and heightened awareness of the madness of the human mind. We are more aware than ever that our old ways of doing things are not working for us. Our old assumptions about who we are, our dualistic way of thinking, our us-and-them mentality have not led to peace—peace in the world at large or peace within ourselves. Quite the opposite. Wars, genocide, oppression, and violence are still going on at this very moment. The world's financial system is on the brink of collapse (and some would say it already *has* collapsed), and the greatest superpowers are in terrible debt. Ecological disaster looms on the horizon. And humans are experiencing record-high levels of depression, anxiety, and stress.

The world has always been mad, but these days, we are more aware of that madness. For the first time in human history, information about the state of the world is available to pretty much everybody who can get access to a computer. It's also probably true to say that we are more desperate than ever for a way out.

This book is not about solving all the problems on the planet; I am not qualified to talk about that. What I do want to talk about is where all human suffering, conflict, and violence originate: the dualistic split in present experience, in the separation of "me" from life itself. If, at some point, each of us does not face our own present experience and heal the madness and violence and separation there, we have no hope of finding a way out of the collective madness of humanity. If we can find out where the violence, the suffering, the separation from life and each other begin in our own experience, and if we can clearly see and understand the suffering we create for ourselves, then we will also be able to see how we create suffering for others, for the ones we love, for our cities, our countries, our continents, our planet.

Violence begins and ends with *you*. Recognizing this truth leads to total responsibility, in the best sense of the word.

I'm not offering a way out of the madness of the human mind, but a way in. I'm not actually offering a solution to suffering, but another way of looking at suffering—a radical new way of *relating* to it. We have no hope of ending suffering—personal or global—until we understand what suffering really is, at the most fundamental level. And when we truly understand suffering, we may discover that true freedom is found not through escaping present experience, but by diving fearlessly into its hidden depths. In there, perhaps, we will discover all the peace, love, and deep acceptance that we were always seeking "out there."

Now, it might sound selfish or narcissistic to focus on your own suffering in this way. "Who am I to sit here and look at my own suffering? Shouldn't I forget about myself, get out there, and help to end the suffering in the world?" Remember, any suffering within you will inevitably get projected out into the world. You and the world are one, as we will discover. Anything you are at war with in yourself, you will eventually go to war with in the world. If there is violence and separation alive in you, you will bring it into your close relationships, into your family, into your workplace, into the world at large. The world is nothing but your projection of it, as spiritual teachers, saints, sages, and mystics throughout the ages have been reminding us.

The spiritual teacher Osho spoke about the paradox of looking deeply into your own experience rather than trying to end all the world's problems: "Yes, it will appear as selfishness. But is the lotus selfish when it blossoms? Is the sun selfish when it shines?" In a very strange way, in order to be totally unselfish, you must be totally selfish, totally obsessed with yourself, but not in the way we usually think of obsession or self. You must be fascinated, curious, willing to see through separation, in all its forms, in the midst of your present experience. You must be open to exploring suffering—how and why it manifests in you, where it originates. You must be willing to take a look at your worst fears, your pain, your sadness, your deepest unfulfilled longings. You must be willing to face them head on and to find the place where even the most seemingly unacceptable aspects of yourself can be deeply accepted.

Great freedom lies in fearlessly facing the darkness and finally coming to see that darkness is inseparable from light.

It lies in recognizing that what you were always seeking was hidden even in your worst fears. To paraphrase Thomas Hardy, if there is a way toward the better, it lies in taking a full look at the worst—and finding deep acceptance there.

When you understand how suffering manifests in you, you immediately understand how it manifests in everyone else. We often focus so much on our individual differences that we fail to see that, in the most basic ways, we are all the same. We all suffer, and we all seek a way out of suffering, as the Buddha taught. When you see and understand the mechanics of suffering in yourself, you gain deep compassion for others' suffering—in the true sense of the word *compassion* (from *com-passio;* literally, "I suffer with").

When I see pain as mine, I am lost in my personal bubble of suffering and feel disconnected from life, shut off and lonely in my misery. But beyond the personal story of my own suffering, I discover that pain is not really my pain. It is the world's pain. It is humanity's pain. When I lose my father, the grief I experience is not my grief, but every son's grief. I grieve for, and with, every son who has ever lost a father. When my partner leaves me, I become anyone who has ever lost someone they love. In the most intimate recesses of present experience, I discover that I *am* the universe that I am trying so hard to save; I discover that I *am* the compassion that I try so hard to act out in the world. I discover that I *am* the others I long so much for connection with. In the depths of the personal, in the midst of the most intensely painful and intimately personal experiences,

I discover the impersonal truth of existence, and there, I am free. Many spiritual teachings speak of escaping the personal and reaching some future impersonal state, but as we shall see in this book, the personal and impersonal are intimately one and cannot be divided in this way. Division is the root of all suffering and conflict.

On one level, this book is not necessary. You are already complete as you are. You are life itself and always have been. *This is it*—here and now! This moment is all there is, and it is complete in itself. There is nothing else to do. Congratulations! You can put down this book and have a cup of tea and a sandwich.

On another level, perhaps you don't yet *recognize* that you are already complete. Perhaps beautiful, inspiring spiritual truths like "You are already complete" and "There is only Oneness" are still just beautiful, inspiring *words* and are not yet a living, experiential *reality* for you. Perhaps you are still battling with your feelings, with pain, with addiction, with relationship conflicts. Perhaps you are still looking for answers, looking for love, looking for approval, looking for enlightenment. Perhaps you are still waiting for peace, still longing to find a way to live in this world in a more grounded, loving, authentic way. Perhaps, even though you *believe* that you are not separate from life, you still *feel* separate from life.

Your suffering is not a curse, a punishment, an aberration, or a sign of your failure in any way. Suffering is always a great place to start exploring present experience. God knows, if I hadn't suffered the way I did, I would never have begun questioning everything I knew and discovering freedom in everything I was at war with, in everything I tried to deny in myself.

I'm not promising you a special state or a special spiritual experience; I'll leave that to the spiritual gurus. Besides, states and experiences come and go, and if we are truly interested in ending suffering, we must go beyond passing states and experiences, beyond spiritual highs, and discover something that doesn't come and go. Something that's always here. Something that's here right now, but always seems to be ignored as we constantly pursue future experiences and long to return to past glories.

I don't see myself as a spiritual or self-help guru; as a special, awakened, or enlightened being; or as fundamentally different from you in any way. I see myself more as a friend, gently pointing you back to who you really are, reminding you of what, deep down, you already know. I certainly don't want you to simply believe everything I tell you. I want you to look for yourself, to test everything I say against your own experience. I am not an authority on life. (Who can be an authority on the birds singing, on the heart beating, on the rain falling, on this moment as it is?) But perhaps the words in this book will point you back to an awareness of what is really true in your experience right now. Perhaps they will point you back to a deep, all-pervading acceptance, ease, and rest at the heart of everything, which will take you beyond the need for any external authority and leave you standing free, like a tree in a storm, facing life head on, fully engaged with the realities and challenges of relative existence, but also grounded in the unshakeable certainty of who you really are, deeply rooted in a *knowing* that will never die.

Why Do We Suffer?

We shall not cease from exploration
And the end of all our exploring
Will be to arrive where we started
And know the place for the first time.

T. S. ELIOT, "Little Gidding"

For most of my life, I was a very sad and lonely little me, a depressed wave in the cosmic ocean of life, feeling totally separate from that ocean, deeply at war with myself and with others, never experiencing a moment's rest. For many years, I tried desperately to fit in, to succeed, to connect with others, to find love, to find my place in the world, but despite my best efforts, I fell into a deeper and deeper depression. I blamed everything and everyone for the way I felt—my genes, my brain chemistry, my upbringing, my parents, my friends, my boss, the cruelty of life, our money-obsessed society, the media, meat eaters, politicians, corporations, the "evildoers." My misery had nothing to do with me, or so I believed. It was the only possible response to a life that had turned against me. Life was cruel, life was unfair, life was unkind, life had cursed me. I blamed life for my misery, and I felt that I had every right to. "If

---

19

you'd experienced what I've experienced, you'd feel this way too!"—that's how I liked to justify my misery to others.

Life had not lived up to my expectations, other people had let me down, and no matter how hard I tried, I just couldn't control the way my life was going. As a result, I had ended up in bed, unable to get up, feeling suicidal, nauseous, and weighed down, unable and unwilling to face each day. What was the point of getting out of bed? Outside my bedroom door there was just more misery waiting for me. I knew what life was, and I wanted to avoid it at all costs. Life was pain, and I didn't want to experience pain.

How had I ended up like this? To put it very simply, over the course of my life, I had built up many ideas about *how life should be.* I had collected many beliefs about reality, many assumptions about the way things really were, many concepts about what should and shouldn't happen in the world. I had come to many conclusions about what was right and what was wrong, what was good and what was evil, what was normal and what was abnormal, what was proper and what was improper.

And I had many *images* of myself that I had been trying to uphold, many demands regarding how I wanted to be seen and how I wanted to see myself. I wanted to see myself, and to be seen, as successful and attractive and intelligent and kind and good and compassionate and talented. But life kept getting in the way of these demands. Life simply wouldn't let me be who I wanted to be. Life just didn't understand me. People just didn't *get* me. Nobody would ever understand me! My frustrated expectations of life and my constant judgments of myself brought pain, and I hated the pain and didn't want to experience it any longer.

However, in my mid-twenties, through a series of ever-deepening insights, I came to see clearly that my depression, at the most basic level, was actually the experience of my own *deep resistance* to life. I was not experiencing something outside of myself called depression. Something called depression was not happening to me. I was experiencing my own inner war with the way things were. And at the root of this war was my own ignorance of *who I really was*. I had stopped seeing the completeness of life; I had forgotten my true nature, and I had gone on the warpath with present experience. Not realizing who I really was, and therefore identifying as a separate "self," I had gone to war with the present moment.

My depression had everything to do with the way I saw the world—with my judgments of it, with my beliefs about it, with my demands about how this moment should be. Underneath my attempt to control life through thinking was my fear of change, of loss, and, ultimately, of death. My resistance to life took me to the extreme—suicidal depression—but we are *all* shut off from wholeness to a greater or lesser extent. The degree to which we shut ourselves off from wholeness is the degree to which we suffer. I had shut myself off totally from life, and the suffering had become unbearable. I was a walking corpse, but life had not made me one. I had innocently turned myself into one, *in my pursuit of a future wholeness that was never going to come.*

At the root of my depression was the sense that I was a separate person—an individual me, an entity separate from life itself and divided from this moment. That individual me had to somehow hold up, support, and sustain something called "my life"—to orchestrate it, to make it go the way I wanted it to, to be in control of it. That's what I had been taught since I was very young, and that's what the world had been screaming at me: I was supposed to be in control of my life; I had to know what I wanted and be able to go out and get it. Everyone else seemed to know who they were, what they were doing, where they were going, but I didn't seem to be able to hold up my story without being crushed by it. *My depression was my experience of not being able to hold up my own life, and feeling de-pressed (pressed down) by my life as a result.*

I see now that we are *all* pressed down by the weight of our own lives, the weight of our history and our imagined futures. In that sense, we are all depressed to some extent! It's only when it becomes virtually impossible to carry the weight that we call ourselves "depressed" and separate ourselves from others. Although we may not all be clinically depressed, we all walk around with stories about ourselves; we all are trying to make our lives go the way we want them to. And we are all failing on some level to be who we are not.

My suffering took the shape of depression, existential angst, painful shyness, and total lack of intimacy in relationships, but we all suffer in our own way. We all suffer, but either we see suffering as something terrible, to be avoided at all costs, or we see it for what it really is—a clear signpost guiding us back home.

In the midst of my extreme depression another possibility shone through: perhaps my failure to hold up my own life was not actually a disease or a mental illness or a sign of dysfunction or weakness at all. *Perhaps this was not my life to hold up in the first place.* Perhaps I wasn't really who I thought I was. Perhaps true freedom had nothing to do with being a better wave in the ocean, with perfecting my story of myself. Perhaps freedom was all about waking up from the dream that we are separate waves in the first place and embracing all that appears in the ocean of present experience. Perhaps *that* was my job, my true calling in life—to accept present experience deeply, to let go of all ideas of how this moment should be, instead of holding up a false image of myself.

I started to lose interest in pretending to be something I wasn't. I started to lose interest in resisting the present moment. I started to fall in love with present experience. I discovered the deep acceptance inherent in every thought, every sensation, every feeling, and my suffering came crashing down. I realized that there was nothing wrong with me, and there never had been. And I realized that this was also true for every other human being on the planet.

Human suffering can seem so unfathomable, so unmanageable, so confusing—too huge a problem to tackle. Sometimes suffering seems so meaningless and so inexplicable, or it appears so randomly or so out of the blue that all that's left is to say, "There must be something wrong with me" or "It's just the way I am" or "It's my fate to suffer like this" or "It must be genetic or have to do with my brain chemicals."

I don't believe that there's anything fundamentally wrong with anyone, that anyone has to suffer, that any misery is pre-destined or built into us in any way.

What I do see is that many people are *seeking*. They are trying to escape what they think and feel in the moment. They are deeply resisting present experience, *but they don't realize this is what they are doing*. So it feels like suffering is just hap-pening to them, almost as if it came from outside of them and they are victims of it. If they did realize the extent of their resistance to the moment, they would no longer have to use all sorts of strange theories to explain or justify their suffer-ing. They would no longer blame life, blame themselves, blame others, or blame circumstances for their suffering. They would no longer blame the alignment of the planets or stars, electro-magnetic forces or cosmic energies, their karma, their guru, or God or the devil for their suffering. They would be responsible in the true sense of the word—able to respond to life as it is right now, as opposed to life as they imagine it is or should be.

All my suffering turned out to be a blessing, not a curse. The depression was there to show me—in the most dramatic way possible—how much I was shutting myself off from life. Seen in this way, suffering is always, always a signpost point-ing back to wholeness.

It's often only when we start hurting that we start listen-ing to life. And somehow we are all provided with the exact amount of suffering we need to recognize who we really are.

Every wave is a unique expression of the ocean, and every wave will suffer in a unique way. Your suffering is your unique invitation back to the ocean.

My depression was pointing directly to spiritual awakening. My depression ("de-pressed") was pointing back to who I really am, which is always deeply at rest ("deep rest"). It was an invitation to let go of my heavy story about the past and future and rest deeply in present experience. It was an invitation to wake up from the dream of separation. It just took me a while to accept that invitation.

Seeing that nothing outside of ourselves really causes our suffering is the key to incredible freedom. Circumstances can never really cause our suffering; it is always in our response to circumstances that we suffer. We suffer only when we seek, when we try to escape certain aspects of our present experience and, in doing so, separate ourselves from life and go to war with ourselves and with others—sometimes in obvious ways, sometimes in very subtle ways. Our suffering is rooted in our unwillingness to feel what we feel, to experience what we are experiencing right now. Suffering is there in our war with life as it is. It is there in our failure to see that everything in the moment is always accepted, in the deepest sense.

There is a lot of confusion over the word *acceptance,* so before we go any further, I want to say a few words about it. One of the first reactions I get from people new to this message is, "Jeff, is your message all about accepting everything—sitting back from life, doing nothing, giving up on the possibility of changing anything? If we simply accept everything that happens, doesn't that lead to passivity, detachment, inaction, and powerlessness?"

Acceptance doesn't mean that we should give up all our attempts to prevent bad things happening, as if that were possible. And I'm not saying we should simply sit back and let bad things happen if we can do something about them. Nobody wants their loved ones to get ill. Nobody wants to lose all their money or be injured in a car crash. Nobody wants their partner to walk out on them suddenly. Nobody wants to be physically attacked. But these things happen. Life doesn't always go according to our plans. Even when we maintain the best of intentions; make the most solid plans; engage in all our positive thinking, prayers, and attempts to manifest our destiny; follow our spiritual paths and promote our spiritual evolution, things happen that we wouldn't have chosen to happen, and we get to see, time and time again, that ultimately we are not in control of this thing we call life. Even the most so-called enlightened people have ended up in a hospital bed, in tremendous pain from a tumor, asking for more morphine.

What I'm saying is that if we are to be truly free, we must face this reality with open eyes. We must move away from denial, wishful thinking, and hope, and tell the truth about life as it is. Great freedom lies in *admitting the truth of this moment,* however much it clashes with our hopes, dreams, and plans.

I'm saying that, ultimately, reality itself—not what we think about reality— is the authority. Acceptance is all about seeing reality, seeing things as they actually are, not as we hope or wish them to be. And from that place of total alignment with what is, all creative, loving, and intelligent action flows naturally.

We are constantly judging life. Things happen, and then we approve or disapprove. We accept or reject. We say, "This should have happened" or "That shouldn't have happened." We say, "Life is bad" or "Life is good" or "Life is meaningless" or "Life is cruel." We say, "Life is always kind to me," or we say, "Life never gives me what I want." But life itself comes *before* all of these labels; it comes before all our judgments about life. Life cannot be good or bad. Life is simply life, appearing as all there is, as what we call good and what we call bad. Life "makes the sun shine on the good and bad alike," as the Bible says. It makes the sun shine, and it is the sun shining, and it is everything the sun shines on, including all the stuff we'd rather the sun didn't shine on.

Later, I will be talking much more about the true nature of acceptance in this deeper sense. But for now, let's just say that from a place of deep acceptance of the way things are, in seeing the inherent perfection of life itself, one is still *totally free* to do what one is moved to do—to help, to change things, to make a difference. It's just that our actions are no longer coming from the root assumption that *reality is broken and needs to be fixed* and, underneath that, the assumption that *each of us is separate from life.* Any movement that comes from the assumption that life is broken will simply perpetuate the disease it promises to cure.

This book is not about sitting back from life and doing nothing; that is detachment, which is another form of separation. This book is about *intimacy with* all life, which you could say is the death of detachment. A passive attitude toward life is not possible when you realize that you *are* life itself.

Awakening is not the end of engagement with life—it is just the beginning. Paradoxically, when we realize how perfect life is, how everything happens exactly as it should, we are freer than ever to go out into the world and change things for the better. In seeing how perfect somebody is, exactly as they are, you are freer than ever to help them take a look at what *they* perceive as imperfection. You're no longer coming from the root assumption that they are a broken thing that needs fixing. You see that they are already whole. And out of the depths of that realization, you point back to their inherent wholeness. *Rooted in wholeness, you are free to fully engage with the dance of apparent separation.*

When you're no longer trying to fix life, perhaps you can be a great help to life. When you're no longer trying to fix other people, perhaps you can be a great blessing to them. Perhaps true healing happens when you get out of the way.

Perhaps that's what life needs more than anything—people who no longer see problems, but who see the inseparability of themselves and the world and who *fully engage* with the world from that place of deep acceptance. Deep acceptance of things as they are and fearless engagement with life are one and the same, however paradoxical that sounds to the rational mind.

COMPLETING OURSELVES IN THE FUTURE

In the novel *The Road* by Cormac McCarthy, a father and a son, ragged and starving, travel together across a post-apocalyptic America. The trees and flowers are dying. Most human beings are dead, and a large number of the living have turned to cannibalism. What keeps father and son going is the hope of something better in the *future*. One of their few possessions is a torn and tattered map. They don't really know where to go; they only know that they need to head south. They don't know what they'll find in the south, or whether there is anything to find there. They just know that they have to keep going south. *South* has come to represent everything beautiful, good, and true in life.

I won't give away the plot, but in the end, it turns out that if they had been a little more aware of what was happening along the way, of what life was trying to show them, time and time again, then they wouldn't have been so eager to reach their destination. In fixating on the destination, they missed the journey, which was where life and love really were.

This story is a wonderful metaphor for how we all live. We are always trying to get *there*, when *here* is where all of life is. We are all trying to get home, when perhaps, just perhaps, we are already home, in our present experience, but don't realize it.

This dynamic plays out in so many of our novels, plays, movies, myths, and spiritual stories. Characters often journey far away from home, discover who they really are, and then return home, somehow changed, somehow the same. In *The Wizard of Oz*, perhaps the most beloved movie of all time, a young girl leaves her colorless home; goes on an incredible, colorful journey; meets various facets of herself; and returns to the same place—only then she sees what's *really* there. Home has not changed, but her eyes have opened to it. At the beginning of many Disney musicals, the main character, feeling like an outcast in their own home, will sing a song about their longing for adventure, for love, for something they can't seem to get at home. That something calls them away, but in the end, they return home, or they find a new home—their true home, their true place in the world. It has been suggested that on the most basic level *every* story shares this common structure: our hero moves from the known to the unknown, but he always returns home in the end. The spiritual seeker leaves home in search of enlightenment and returns home again only to discover that the enlightenment he sought was there from the beginning.

In music, notes and chords go on a similar journey, moving away from their natural homes, creating tension for the captivated listener, but finally resolving themselves by returning to their starting points. And we, the listeners, feel like the music *moved* us in some way, taking us on a journey away from the ordinary and returning us—somehow changed, touched, transformed—to where we were. We were moved, even though we didn't move at all.

We feel compelled to leave home in search of whatever it is that will make us feel complete, but we also feel equally compelled to return home. After a long, exhausting day at kindergarten or at the office, we just want to go home—back to mother and father, back to our loved ones, back to sleep. As children, we get homesick when we are away from home for too long, away from the ones we love. When people die, we say they have "gone home" or found a new home where they can rest eternally, and finally be at peace.

Throughout all human history, the search for home has expressed itself in every single facet of our lives—in our art, our music, our science, our mathematics, our literature, our philosophy, our quest for love, our spirituality. The search for home goes very, very deep in the human psyche.

In art, the interplay of the seeker and the sought, foreground and background, light and shade, positive and negative space creates tension, drama. A joke seeks a punch line. A sentence seeks completion. It is our built-in longing for resolution that makes a piece of art, a joke, a sentence so compelling, so dramatic, so satisfying. Perhaps it is that same longing that has driven mathematicians, philosophers, physicists, for all human history, to seek some kind of grand, unified, all-encompassing theory of reality, to find wholeness in the chaos, to find love in the midst of devastation, to find cosmic closure. We are told that even the universe is expanding and contracting—somehow seeking equilibrium, seeking home. All things long to come to rest.

Home is not a place, a thing, or a person. It is rest. At its root, the word *home* means "to rest" or "to lie down."

We are like waves in the ocean, longing to return to the ocean that we never left. A wave experiences itself as *separate* from the ocean and, from that place of primal misidentification, begins to seek the ocean, in a million different ways. It is seeking itself and doesn't realize it. Its longing for home is its longing for itself. This is the human condition.

How does this sense of separateness manifest in our present experience? Well, we live with that nagging feeling that something is *missing* from our lives, don't we? It's a feeling of lack, a strange empty feeling, like there's a hole in us that needs to be filled up, like we are not good enough as we are, like there is something fundamentally wrong with us. It's out of this basic sense of emptiness that we go off into the world of time and space in search of our true home, in search of cosmic rest, in search of relief, in search of the fullness of things. We seek fulfillment, the filling-up of emptiness. In our cosmic homesickness, we seek union with God, with Spirit, with nature, with a guru. We seek full bellies and full bank accounts. Feminine and masculine seek each other, trying to complete themselves through union; we seek our soul mates, our other halves who will complete us. We seek our destiny, not realizing that we are already living it.

Out of a basic sense of incompleteness, we begin our search for a future completeness. Not recognizing our true identity as the ocean of present experience, we begin to seek that ocean, and we truly believe that we will find it in the future, in the "one day." We say to ourselves, "I am incomplete now, but *one day*, once I've found what I'm looking for, I'll be complete."

"One day I'll find love, and then I'll be complete. One day I'll become spiritually enlightened, and then I'll be complete. One day

I'll be a success, and then I'll be complete. One day I'll be rich. One day I'll get healed. One day they'll approve of me. One day I'll be fully present. One day I'll be completely conscious. One day I'll be living in the Now. One day I'll find peace. One day I'll be fully myself. One day I'll be understood. One day I'll be a star. One day they'll love and accept me. One day I'll be fully spiritually evolved. One day I'll be a father or a mother. One day I'll be free. One day I'll be happy. Yes, I'll be complete, one day. But not yet. Not yet."

We seek wealth, power, love, success, and enlightenment in the future, in the "one day," because these things symbolize home to us. We think that getting what we want, finding what we are looking for, will take us home. Our cosmic homesickness is the root of everything.

Sometimes we even get what we want—the new car, the new relationship, the new job, the slim and toned body, the new spiritual experience, the fame, the adulation, the success. And we feel whole and complete for a while. But soon that empty, unfulfilled feeling returns, and the seeking starts up again. It's as if there is something in us that is perpetually unsatisfied with what is; it always wants *more*. No matter how much it gets, it wants *more*. No matter how much it owns, or achieves, or possesses, it wants *more*. No matter how many experiences it has, no matter how much it adds to itself, it wants *more*.

No matter how complete the story of my life is, it could always be more complete. The job could always pay more; the relationship could always be more fulfilling; I could always have more money, more success, more adulation. The spiritual experience could always be deeper, longer. I could always be closer to enlightenment or more enlightened, more present, more conscious, more free, more loved. Or there could be less of what I don't want—less pain, less fear, less sadness, less anger, less suffering, less ego, fewer thoughts. The story of my life will never be complete, which is to say, I will never complete myself in time.

I knew a man who was a millionaire before he was forty. He worked hard and got what he always wanted—more money than he could ever need; a big, luxurious house; a beautiful, loving partner; adorable, intelligent, obedient, hard-working kids; lots of friends; adulation; respect. He retired at thirty-seven. Quite literally the day after he retired, he was sitting alone at home, and suddenly that empty, incomplete, homesick feeling resurfaced—the same feeling he had felt as a teenager, the same feeling that had driven him to work himself nearly to death in order to make his millions, the same feeling he had spent his life trying to escape. It was the feeling that the money, the big house, the wife, and the family were *supposed* to take away. That's what the world had promised.

Now he had a big problem. He had what he wanted, and he *still* wasn't complete. He still felt homesick. What was wrong with him? Well, now he didn't have the distraction of work. Now, faced again with the lack, he had no way of escaping it.

That evening, the young millionaire took a drink. And another. And another. Very soon he was dependent on the drinks. His addiction to work was replaced with an addiction to alcohol. After all, his sense of cosmic lack had to be obliterated somehow.

This man's story is the perfect example of how the seeker cannot be satisfied, even when it gets what it wants. The basic sense of lack we experience cannot be removed by anything in the world of time and space. Getting what you want does not take away your primal homesickness.

And there is another problem, one the Buddhists have always known: in a world that is totally impermanent, in a world of flux and change, in a world that is ultimately beyond your control, even if you do get what you want, you can then *lose what you have.* Ultimately, there is no security in life. What appears always disappears.

We know, deep down, that nothing, absolutely nothing, can protect us from the possibility of losing what we have, and this is why we experience so much anxiety in our lives. Now that we have the new house, we worry about losing our job and not being able to keep up payments. Now that we have plenty of money in our bank account, we worry about the economy collapsing and our savings being wiped out. However happy you are in your relationship with your partner, you worry about her leaving you, getting ill, or worse. You worry about your kids being hurt. You worry about your own body, about all the things that could go wrong with it. And you know that nothing—not your big house, the furniture, the fancy car, the swimming pool, all of that money in your bank account, not even your beloved spiritual guru—can protect you from loss, from change, from flux, from the way of things.

Sure, people and objects can give you the temporary feeling of security, comfort, and pleasure, but they cannot give you what you really long for—which is freedom from all loss, freedom from lack, and ultimately freedom from death. They cannot give you the cosmic security you crave; they cannot bring you home. Nothing outside of yourself can bring you home.

Here's another way of thinking about our search for home. Imagine you're a newborn baby. You've never seen the world before; everything is unfamiliar and mysterious to you. All of those strange sights, sounds, and smells! All of those strange feelings and sensations that you have no name for yet! You wake up in the middle of the night. You're alone and hungry and scared (although you don't have words for any of these feelings yet). On some level you feel *not okay,* and you have no way of communicating this except through crying and screaming. You can't say, "Excuse me! I don't feel okay! Please come to my aid, someone!" You can only scream and wait for help to come.

Your mother comes in and holds you and soothes you and feeds you. Suddenly, everything feels okay again. Suddenly, the discomfort doesn't seem so bad. The fear doesn't seem so bad. You are no longer alone. You feel safe again. You feel protected by forces outside yourself. Your *not okay* has turned to *okay.* Something outside of you came and made things okay again.

If the baby could talk he or she might say something like this: "When the *not okay* feeling comes, I scream. Eventually Mummy comes, and then the *not okay* goes away, like magic.

Mummy takes away the *not okay*. Mummy makes the *not okay* go away."

But it wasn't really Mother who made things okay. Mother doesn't really have the power to take away the *not okay* feelings—that's just what it must seem like to a newborn baby. It's a beautiful illusion—*that objects, people, or anything outside of ourselves can make us okay,* can bring us home. We very quickly start to believe that looking for something outside of ourselves eventually will take away all the bad thoughts, sensations, and feelings. The seeking mechanism is set up, probably from a very early age. We look outside of ourselves for something to make things okay. Perhaps our attachment to our mothers is the first expression of our seeking. But it's not really Mother that we are attached to—it is home. For most babies, I would imagine that their mother is the first person who symbolizes home.

I wonder if, in a million different ways, with all our seeking, we're just trying to get back to the womb, the place of non-separation. In the womb, there was no separation between me and the womb, no separation between me and Mother. There was simply wholeness, without an inside or outside. In the womb, there was no "other." In other words, *everything* was the womb. It's like the whole world was there, the whole universe was there, just to take care of me, just to protect me. I was embraced in an ocean of love, always. It was home, without opposite, because in the womb I had no conception of inside and outside. It was the ocean in which every single wave of experience was deeply, deeply accepted. It was myself.

In fact, I wasn't even *in* the womb—I *was* the womb. That's how complete it was. It was not me *and* the womb (two things); it was just the womb (one thing, everything). And so, in truth, I did not come out of the womb. In my deepest essence, I was—and am—the womb. I am the wholeness that I long for.

But from this place of total, ever-present completeness with no opposite, it seems as though I was ejected without warning. Suddenly, all of that effortless security was gone. Suddenly, I was faced with a world of things, a world of separate objects, a contingent world, a place where comfort, security, and safety—okayness—could appear and disappear at any moment. It was no longer a world of permanent okayness. It was now a world where okayness battled with not-okayness.

It is not unreasonable to suggest that since every human being that exists or that has ever existed has at one time been in the womb, we may all still carry a vague, preverbal memory of a deep sense of okayness, and we may all have a yearning to return there. Perhaps our search for home is also our search for the womb—not the physical location, but the wholeness that was there. We long to feel safe, protected, at one with everything. We long to be deeply okay again.

As adults, we no longer literally scream for our mothers; instead, we seek relief from discomfort in more sophisticated ways. We metaphorically scream for the next cigarette, the next drink, the next sexual conquest, the next job promotion, the next spiritual experience, the next *release*—anything to make things okay, anything to take away the not okay.

Even children who have the most idyllic, loving upbringings do not escape this basic feeling of separation, of lack. It seems to be built into the experience of being an individual. No parents are guilty of creating this sense of separation, this sense of lack; nobody is intentionally turning their children into seekers. Newborn organisms capable of abstract thought naturally come to seek a conceptual completeness in the future. They naturally begin to build up all sorts of ideas about what is okay and what is not okay in their experience, and try to escape everything they come to perceive as not okay, in order to reach a place of okay. Seen from this angle, developing a sense of separation, and then seeking to correct it by finding wholeness, is part of the natural evolution of life. Seeking is not a mistake, and it is not the enemy. It is simply a case of mistaken identity.

PRESENT-MOMENT RESISTANCE

I will be complete . . .
> *when I finally fit in with my peer group, with my work*
>   *colleagues, with society.*
> *when people finally understand me and approve of what I do.*
> *when everybody around me changes.*
> *when I've created a masterpiece that everybody adores.*
> *when my body is perfect.*
> *when I've finally manifested my destiny.*
> *when I've found my soul mate.*
> *when I'm fully awakened.*

when I win the gold medal.

when I have a child.

when I've finally found what I'm looking for.

We look to the future for completeness, because on some level we feel incomplete in the present moment.

You want to be understood in the future? It means that on some level you feel misunderstood now. You want enlightenment in the future? It means that on some level you feel unenlightened now. You want love in the future? It means that on some level you feel unloved right now. *The question "What are you seeking in the future?" is identical with the question "What are you running away from right now?"*

It is crucial to understand this: our search for something abstract in the future—enlightenment, wealth, power, success, love—is always deeply rooted in present-moment resistance. Our search for future completeness is always rooted in an experience of present incompleteness. Present-moment incompleteness is where all our suffering and seeking begin. And a deep acceptance of the present moment is where it can end.

Sometimes people come to me and ask how they can become enlightened. They believe that I am enlightened (though I would never say I am) and that I can teach them how to become like me. Often I will simply answer, "Well, what do you mean by the word *enlightenment?* When you become enlightened, how will your experience be different from the way it is *right now?*" And often in response they will say something like, "I think that when I become enlightened, my fear will go away. I think my sadness and my pain will disappear. I think enlightenment will take away all the bad things about myself."

You see, nobody really wants to become "enlightened." They want to escape *present* feelings of dissatisfaction, sadness, pain, anger, frustration, boredom, or feelings of being unloved, unwanted, and unfulfilled. They simply want to end their suffering. But instead of facing that suffering head on, right now, and seeing the wholeness within it, they are waiting for a future event or state or experience to come and end it for them. They simply want to come home, as we all do. But in their story, they have fixated on the idea of enlightenment as their future home.

We don't want pain to appear, and yet it appears. We don't want fear to appear, and yet it appears. Because of our conditioning, we don't see pain, fear, sadness, anger, and all kinds of other feelings as part of the completeness, as part of the wholeness of life. We have been conditioned to see parts of our experience as imperfections, contaminations, aberrations, impurities, *expressions of incompleteness.* In other words, we have been taught, trained, even brainwashed, to see some parts of our experience as threats to life itself. We believe that parts of our experience are somehow *against* life—like they don't deserve a place in us. Anger, fear, sadness, discomfort, pain—they should not be allowed in. I reject them because I believe that they don't belong in me. I don't see them as being part of the wholeness of life. I believe that they are dangerous to my well-being. And so I spend my life running away from them.

———————

Which parts of your experience feel like they don't belong? Which thoughts, sensations, feelings feel alien to you? Which ones feel out of place, like they shouldn't be there, like they aren't really you?

Put very simply, we seek purity, perfection, and completeness *outside* of this present experience because we see our present experience as broken, as incomplete, as imperfect, as not whole in some way. We *seek* wholeness because we do not *see* wholeness in this present moment. We do not see the wholeness in these present thoughts, sensations, and feelings, so we look for it in the future. We become seekers of wholeness, and now we require a future to complete ourselves. The seeker always needs time to find what he or she is looking for. The present moment becomes a means to an end.

This is where all suffering begins—the loss of the present moment, the loss of our true home.

TRYING TO CONTROL THIS MOMENT

A man was once speaking to me about his problem with controlling his anger around his children. He said his anger was like a volcano—it would erupt out of nowhere, when he least expected it. He would return home from work, exhausted after a long day at the office, and his kids would be screaming, running around all over the place, making a mess. He would do everything he could to try to calm them down, to make them behave. He'd try every tactic he'd learned over the years—talking nicely to them, reasoning with them, ignoring them, being "present" with them, being firm with them, being "spiritual" with them, rewarding them, punishing them. But nothing worked. They simply wouldn't listen to him, and he would start to feel the anger bubbling up inside of him. He would desperately try to keep his anger at bay; he would try to hold it in, accept it, love it, allow it, transcend it, be "choicelessly aware" of it, repress it, "become" it, but it would always just *explode,* no matter what he did or didn't do. And then he would find himself lashing out at his children, roaring at the top of his lungs, insulting them, saying things he didn't really mean, behaving in a way that he would later regret. His anger seemed to be out of his control.

Sound familiar? Do you sometimes find yourself reacting in ways you don't understand, with your children, your partner, your parents, your friends?

Remember, all examples in this book apply to you. With every example I give, go straight to your own experience and find where it is relevant to your life.

This man had been to some spiritual teachers and shared his problem with them, and they told him things like, "Choose not to be angry" or "There is no choice whether anger appears or not" or "There is only Oneness. Everything is equal, so it doesn't matter whether you get angry with your children or not. Nobody is getting angry." These ideas provided some temporary relief, but they did not ultimately end his suffering. He could see that, ultimately, exploding with rage was simply a part of life and had its place, but that understanding didn't stop it from happening or end his suffering over it. The anger was there, whatever the spiritual teachings said, and it was destroying his relationship with those he loved the most. All the spiritual concepts in the world didn't seem to get to the heart of his problem. It felt like there was nothing he could do, and he just had to learn to tolerate his anger.

I asked the man what he was seeking in the situation, and he couldn't answer. It seemed like the angry outbursts just happened to him. He just couldn't see how his angry outbursts were related to his search for wholeness, to his being at war with present experience. He didn't see himself as someone who was seeking anything. He wasn't looking for enlightenment. He wasn't looking for fame or wealth. It seemed as though he was just responding to a very difficult situation in the best way he could.

Sometimes to find the seeking in a situation you need to stop, take a deep breath, and hold up a magnifying glass to present experience. The man and I started to explore his experience, and with some very simple and honest investigation, it soon became clear that a lot was happening during the few short moments it took him to go from politely asking his kids to settle down to exploding in anger.

As he saw his children screaming and shouting, all sorts of very uncomfortable thoughts and feelings arose—feelings about his own incompetence as a father and his powerlessness in the face of the situation. "What's wrong with me? Why can't I control them? I'm a grown man—I should be able to control the situation. But I can't. I'm failing as a father, failing as a man." Feelings of intense frustration and then despair and total helplessness were appearing, and these feelings began to feel totally overwhelming. The grown man began feeling like a helpless child—not the mature, strong father that he wanted to see himself as. It would begin to feel like his whole identity was crumbling, and a kind of existential panic set in. It was almost as if he were facing his own physical death; in fact, he was facing the death of his self-image as a mature, strong father figure, the death of who he thought he was, who he thought he should be in the moment, who other people thought he was. He was facing the death of the image of himself that he had been living with, the image that he had been projecting onto the world. And this confrontation was provoked simply by his children being a little too loud.

In his helplessness, in his powerlessness, in his panic, he felt the urge to lash out. In his weakness, he wanted to feel strong again. There was something in him that did not want to feel helpless and out of control—especially in the presence of his children!

When you feel totally powerless and unable to control the moment, lashing out and demonstrating power can provide some relief, if only temporarily. Attacking another human being is the perfect way to distract yourself from your own deeply uncomfortable feelings—feelings you simply don't want to allow in yourself. It is often when we feel most helpless (and cannot see our helplessness or admit to ourselves and others that we feel this way) that we become the most irrational, the most violent, and sometimes end up hurting those we love. Instead of allow-ing ourselves to feel hurt, we hurt others. And then we blame them; we tell them they deserved what they got, that they caused the explosion, that they *made* us angry. (And then, if we have picked up nonduality concepts, we tell them that we had no choice!)

At some point in his life, this man learned—as most of us do—that feelings like helplessness and powerlessness are not okay. Feeling unable to control the moment is not okay. Feeling weak is not okay. Feelings like helplessness are associ-ated with lack of safety, with danger, with not being loved or accepted, and ultimately they are associated with death. For many people, the feeling of helplessness is to be avoided at all costs. Much of our suffering comes from deeply unaccepted feelings of helplessness, powerlessness, weakness, insecurity, and uncertainty in the face of this moment.

We could probably boil all our suffering down to this:

I want to control this moment, but I cannot!

This man may not have been seeking enlightenment or fame or glory, but in the moment, he was a desperate seeker. He was urgently seeking to control and escape feelings of weakness and powerlessness in the face of life. In the moment, he became a seeker of power, of control, and ultimately of love. He was seeking an *escape* from what he was experienc-ing. And lashing out at his kids provided, for a moment, the escape, the release he craved.

On the surface, he looked like a father unable to control his anger at his naughty children. But when you look at what the man was actually experiencing, you see someone feeling utterly frustrated, feeling like a total fool and a failure as a father and as a man, feeling powerless and helpless and weak, and desperately seeking a way out of his predicament. And you see someone not able to *admit* any of this, to himself or to his children. Underneath our rage, we will always find unaccepted pain and powerlessness.

Until he saw the seeking that was going on within his experience, the man felt that this suffering was just happening to him—that he was a helpless victim of life, that perhaps he was genetically programmed to get angry, or that his response to his children was cosmically predestined in some way and, thus, there was no hope of change. But by exposing the seeking the way we did, it became clear exactly *why* he was suffering and *how* that suffering was being created. He was simply not allowing himself to feel what he felt, in the moment. He was not allowing himself to feel helpless, even for a moment. He could not see the deep acceptance in his present experience of helplessness.

In coming to *see* what he was running away from (helplessness), he automatically saw that he no longer *needed* to run away from it—that it was okay to feel helpless, that the feeling of helplessness, in that moment, could be totally accepted. (I will talk later about how and why even the most seemingly negative feelings can be accepted.) He had simply never allowed himself to feel truly helpless before, even for a moment (and a moment of helplessness is all you ever have to face); he had always assumed that it was not okay to feel that way. In seeing that it was, in fact, deeply okay to feel helpless, in *this* moment, and that there was even a strange joy and peace in the midst of the helplessness, he no longer felt the urge to escape.

Accepting his feeling of helplessness meant he was no longer a victim of life. Helplessness was no longer controlling him, because it was now *allowed* to appear and disappear in him. And what he discovered was that, in finally allowing himself to feel weak and helpless—totally helpless—he felt less helpless and more in control than ever. Strength is not the opposite of weakness. Real strength lies in the total embrace of weakness. (We will see later how, in truth, there are no opposites in present experience.)

When you *see* what you are seeking, and when you see that what you are trying to escape is deeply okay—that recognition, in itself, is the end of seeking. Seeing is the end of seeking. And there is no next step. No "how to" is then required.

Later, I will discuss in more detail how, in every moment, every single part of your present experience is *already* deeply accepted. But for now, let's simply note that in every experience of suffering, when you take the focus off the details of the situation, off the story of what's happening, off the external circumstances, and really come back to your present experience—to present thoughts, feelings, and sensations in the body—you will always find seeking, even if that seeking is playing out in very subtle ways. You will always find there's something you're not allowing yourself to fully experience, something that is innocently trying to express itself within you, but is being met with fear and resistance. You will always find an invitation to deeply accept this moment, however unacceptable this moment seems.

The Ocean of Acceptance

There is no greater mystery than this, that we keep
seeking reality though in fact we are reality.
RAMANA MAHARSHI

When you bring your attention right back to present experience, to what's actually happening right now, where you are, what do you find? Do you find that anything here is fixed, unchanging, *immovable?* Do you find a separate, enduring *self* here? Do you find anything solid here called *me?* Or do you find that everything here is constantly changing, moving, dancing from moment to moment?

Thoughts appear and disappear, all by themselves. Images, memories, and ideas all pop into awareness, linger for a while, and then disappear. All sorts of feelings come and go—sadness, boredom, frustration, anger, fear. Sensations happen all over the body. Sounds appear out of nowhere—the traffic outside, a television buzzing, a door slamming, your own breathing, a bird chirping. *Tweet tweet!*

Throughout the day, all sorts of thoughts, sensations, feelings, and sounds arise and fall in the ocean of awareness that you are. Everything that appears in awareness we could call a *wave of experience.* A thought is a wave. A sound is a wave. A feeling is a wave. A sensation is a wave. All of these thought waves, sound waves, feeling waves, and sensation waves appear and disappear in the wide-open space of awareness, the vast ocean that you are in your essence.

Can you recognize that your experience of life is *always* simply a present-moment dance of waves, all happening in the vast ocean that you are? (And for *ocean,* you can substitute the word *consciousness* or *awareness* or *being* or *presence*—or whatever word feels right for this reality beyond words. I use these words interchangeably throughout this book. Who you really are doesn't mind what you call it.)

What you are, as the ocean, simply holds all of these little waves of experience as they arise and fall, as they are born and die. Thoughts, sensations, sounds, and feelings come and go in you. You are not your thoughts, not your feelings, not your ideas or judgments of yourself, not the story of your successes or failures, not any of the sensations or sounds that appear and disappear. *And yet,* what you are—as the wide-open space in which all thoughts, sensations, sounds, and feelings are allowed to appear and disappear—is also somehow *inseparable* from those thoughts, sensations, sounds, and feelings. You are not your thoughts, but at the same time *all* thoughts are allowed to come and go in the intimacy that you are. What you are is not sounds, and yet *all* sounds are allowed to appear and disappear in you.

Don't worry if you find these words a bit confusing and paradoxical right now. Throughout the book we will be coming back to this *intimacy,* this *inseparability,* this *nonduality* between what you are and life itself. I will point to this from many different angles and explain it in many different ways.

Now, from the perspective of what you are, from the perspective of the ocean, although the waves are all different in appearance, they are the same in *essence.* They are all water. And so, using this metaphor, you could say the ocean *knows* that all the waves are simply part of itself. Every thought, every feeling, every sensation that appears in you is simply the ocean dancing. From the strong, violent waves to the soft, gentle waves—they are all water. And so, on the deepest level, the ocean does not have a *problem* with any of the waves, because it knows that none of the waves can threaten who it really is. There is, therefore, a deep okayness with all the waves, a peace beyond understanding, which comes from recognizing their basic inseparability from the ocean.

None of the waves of life can harm the ocean of you. None of the waves can destroy you. None of the waves can detract from you, and none of the waves can add to you. None of the waves are alien to you.

And so whether the ocean appears as a thought wave, a pain wave, a fear wave, a sadness wave, a wave of excitement, a wave of joy, or any other wave, the ocean knows that, on the deepest level, all of these appearances are okay. They all have a home in what you are. What you are is vast enough to hold all of them.

As all the authentic spiritual teachers throughout the ages have been reminding us, in reality you are not a separate person, not an individual self, but the open space in which all of the little waves of experience—thoughts, sensations, sounds, feelings—come and go. You are, quite literally, what you seek. You are the consciousness that holds the dance of form. You are the vast expanse of awareness in which the world appears and disappears. No matter what appears and disappears in your experience, you remain the calm in the midst of the storm, the deep, vast ocean that cannot be destroyed by even the most violent wave. The waves may rise and crash, but in the ocean's depths, there is silence—silence and knowing.

You are like the white pages behind these words. You are behind every word in this book—ever present, always there in the background, essential to making the words seen, but rarely noticed and even more rarely appreciated.

I think this is where all religious and spiritual teachings point in the end: to the fact that there is something—call it what you will (for not being an it, it is truly unnamable)— here, right in the depths of present experience, that doesn't come and go, that cannot break or rot or shatter, even in the midst of extreme sadness or pain or fear. It is a place that is always deeply okay, even when things on the surface seem not okay. And being beyond the opposites, beyond the dualistic world of thought, it is beyond the cycle of birth and death. It was never born and cannot die. It is the completeness the separate wave is seeking but can never find. It is *home*.

We are so busy trying to move away from discomfort and pain and reach completeness in the future that we end up missing this present completeness. We are so busy trying to come home that we miss the inescapable fact that we are already home. We are so busy trying to hold up an image of ourselves, trying to prove who we are to ourselves and the world, that we miss that what we are is simply the wide-open space in which *all* images come and go. We are so busy seeking that we end up missing this open space that holds everything, an open space that is *itself* the end of seeking.

You are what you seek, as the great spiritual teachers have always been telling us. And you won't find it in the future. It can only be found now.

WAVE MANAGEMENT

From the perspective of the ocean, nothing is a problem, in the deepest sense. Pain, anger, fear, frustration—they come and go in the ocean, and they are not, in the deepest sense, problems. But as human beings, not recognizing who we really are, we make them into problems. We say: "This wave does not belong in the ocean! It threatens the ocean—it threatens what I am. In some way, it is blocking the completeness of the ocean, and if I could just get rid of it, the completeness will be there again."

What we are essentially doing is not allowing a wave to be in the ocean. We are not allowing a wave, which is already a perfect expression of life, to be there in life! We are so deeply conditioned to judge the waves as good, bad, ugly, beautiful, safe, dangerous, positive, or negative that we end up missing the inherent completeness of every single wave of experience—of every thought, every sensation, every feeling.

We stand in judgment of the waves. On the most basic level, we judge that some waves are okay and some waves are not okay. Some waves are allowed in what we are, and some waves are not allowed. And that's where what we call *resistance* begins. Many spiritual teachers talk about *resistance of the present moment* and how it is at the root of all our psychological suffering. Now we can see *why* we resist a thought or feeling: we resist because we don't see the completeness in it, because on some level, we perceive it as a threat to what we are. We resist out of fear because we don't see the inseparability and intimacy between what we are and what appears in present experience. And so, on some level, we feel that what's happening is not okay, and we move to escape it.

We find very complicated ways to do it, but essentially what we are trying to do is very simple: *get rid of the waves we don't like.* We want to control the ocean by managing the waves, so the waves that appear are only those we want to appear. All human suffering is a variation on this theme—trying to control the waves, trying to control our present-moment experience so it conforms to our ideas and concepts of how it should be. If you want to suffer, compare this moment with your image of how it should be!

I end up running away from any aspect of my present experience that I see as a threat to completeness. I quite literally go to war with myself. I split myself in two, me versus the "bad waves" or the "dangerous waves" or the "dark waves" or the "evil waves" in myself. Certain waves in myself become a *threat*. And so I reach out to the world—for the next cigarette, the next sexual encounter, the next pint of beer, the next spiritual high—in order to no longer feel what I feel, in order to avoid certain waves, and in order to ultimately get rid of this incompleteness, this void, this sense of lack at the center of my being. I become *addicted* (to lovers, to gurus, to substances), attach myself to rigid belief systems, or work myself to death— all so I don't have to experience what I experience, so I don't have to feel what I really feel in this moment, so I can numb myself to the pain of being human. As human beings, we do very complicated, dangerous, and even violent things to escape the discomfort of present experience. But what is happening underneath is always very simple: we are resisting what is.

For a while, the money, the cigarette, the sexual encounter, the spiritual experience seem to provide relief from this predicament; the external object or person appears to take away the sadness, the loneliness, the fear, and provide the completeness I long for. I cling to anything that I think is giving me wholeness. Many spiritual teachings talk about *attachment*, and now we can see why we become attached: when we think these external objects and people are providing us with wholeness, we can't let go of them, because letting go would mean losing wholeness. Hanging onto them can become a matter of life and death.

Later, I'll talk about how we unconsciously give power to those people and objects in our world that we perceive to be giving us wholeness, and in doing so, how we lose our own power and stop trusting in our own experience. In that sense, the seeker always has a guru—something or someone who has power over them. The guru takes many forms—a spiritual guru (who appears to have the power of enlightenment), a lover (who appears to have the power of love), a bottle of beer (which appears to have a mysterious power to make you feel better). The object or person seems to take away your discomfort, for a time. For a short while, the burden of self, the burden of seeking, falls away, and there is a temporary relief from discomfort, from pain, from suffering. When you are around your lover or your spiritual master, or when you are watching your favorite sports team, or when you are in the intimacy of lovemaking, in the thrill of extreme sports, or in the depths of meditation, everything seems *okay* again. The seeking relaxes, and for a while, there is relief from the burden of being a separate wave.

But here's the problem: when you withdraw the alcohol, the spiritual teacher, the lover, the activity, the discomfort reappears again, sometimes with a vengeance. When you take away the sought-after object—the addiction object, the thing you imagined was completing you—the seeking returns. It's often only when you lose what you thought was completing you that you become aware of the seeking that was bubbling underneath. You simply didn't realize that you were using your "guru" to complete you. The seeking was unconscious.

Yes, it's easy to believe that you're free from seeking when things are going well for you, when you have what you want and life is good. You say, "I don't need anything to complete me! I am complete!" But then you lose your money, your possessions, your health, your partner, your spiritual guru, your fame, your success, your looks, your memory of your enlightenment experience—the object or person or experience that you thought was completing you. And the resulting incompleteness, the resulting loneliness, the deep dissatisfaction with life—everything that your "powerful" objects or people were supposed to take away—resurfaces. The object, the person, the passing experience didn't really have any power—at least, not the power you really longed for: the power to remove seeking, once and for all.

Yes, often we don't realize we are seeking until we experience *loss*. Loss can be a terrible thing, or it can be a real opportunity to see that, to be complete, you never needed what you thought you needed.

What do you think you need to be complete? What do you fear losing? What, if you lost it, would make you incomplete?

True freedom does not depend on any external source. True freedom is the freedom from dependency on outside sources to complete you. The cigarette, the sexual encounters, the loving gaze of a guru cannot free you permanently. Only when your attention turns 180 degrees to look at the not-okay waves that you are running away from is there the possibility of discovering total freedom and peace within your own experience.

THE TRUE MEANING OF ACCEPTANCE

Let's go deeper into the idea of *acceptance*—a word that seems to be very much misunderstood.

Now, we could say that what you are, as the ocean, accepts every wave, simply because it *is* every wave. It has no choice but to accept! The ocean does not accept some waves and reject others; this is an *unconditional* acceptance that is way beyond our conditioned ideas about acceptance. The ocean's acceptance of its waves is beyond the conceptual opposites of acceptance and nonacceptance. The acceptance is the *inseparability* of the ocean and the waves, and as such, it has no opposite. Every wave is *already accepted* by the ocean, and it is this already-accepted nature of the waves that goes to the heart of what this book is all about. This is the deepest acceptance of life, which you as an individual cannot achieve.

Actually, it's not a question of trying to *achieve* this deepest acceptance; it's a question of recognizing it, seeing it, noticing it in every single experience. You don't have to achieve this deepest acceptance; it has already happened, and what's left is to simply and effortlessly *notice* that it has already happened, in this moment and in every moment. Every wave of experience—every thought, every sensation, every feeling, every sound, every smell—is already allowed to be here. By the time a wave appears, it has *already been accepted* by what you are. The arrival of a wave *is* its acceptance. The floodgates are already open; this moment has already been allowed in, exactly as it is right now. *We are only ever experiencing what has already been allowed!*

What you are has already accepted the present moment, exactly as it is. What you are has already said yes to what is, otherwise what is appearing would not be appearing. What you are cannot resist anything that is appearing now, for it *is* everything appearing now. Everything is simply irresistible to what you are.

So when I talk about acceptance, I'm not using the word in the way we have been conditioned to use it. I'm using the word in a new way, one that points to this deepest acceptance of life—an acceptance, an allowing, that has *already happened*. And so when I suggest that you accept or allow what is, it's a shorthand way of directing your attention to the fact that, in this moment, these thoughts, sensations, feelings, sights, sounds, and smells must have already been allowed in, because they are already appearing!

To accept thoughts and feelings is to simply, gently, effortlessly notice that, in this moment, those thoughts and feelings are already accepted, that they have already been allowed in. They are already here. Accepting is not a time-bound achievement, but a never-ending present-moment reality.

You cannot accept—for what you are is acceptance itself. You are not really a separate person—you are an effortless yes *to this moment.*

This definition turns many spiritual teachings on their head. Now acceptance is not a state to reach in the future. It's not something to look for, wait for, hope for, beg for. It's not a personal achievement or something that comes through years of effort. It's not a magical event, a transformation of consciousness, or energetic shift that will happen one day. It's not a task. It's not spiritual homework. It's something to rediscover, *right in the midst of your present experience,* here and now, no matter what is happening. Acceptance is not a future goal; it is a present reality, always. If it is grace, then it is an ever-present grace, available to all, all of the time.

This definition totally revolutionizes our understanding of acceptance and rejection. Acceptance is no longer about me, a separate individual, trying to accept, trying to be in a state of constant acceptance, trying to reach acceptance as a future goal, trying to live up to some unreachable ideal of acceptance promoted by spiritual teachers and gurus. That is another form of seeking. Acceptance is about recognizing yourself as the open space of acceptance, as the ocean that already accepts all its waves, unconditionally here and now—including any wave of nonacceptance.

I remember years ago, when I saw myself as a spiritual seeker, hungry for the release and escape of enlightenment, I used to believe that accepting, or "doing acceptance," 24 hours a day, 7 days a week, 365 days a year, was the key to becoming enlightened. If I could just accept everything all the time, I would be free, or so I thought. It was a beautiful idea, but no matter how much I tried to accept everything, to be present with everything, to allow everything unconditionally, to be choicelessly aware of everything, there were still some things I just could not accept. Extreme physical pain, rape, torture, genocide—how could I accept all of this? When extreme pain happened in my own experience, I would try desperately to accept it, but would exhaust myself along the way, and then punish myself for my own failure to live up to what I thought I was supposed to live up to.

I realize now that there was an agenda (in other words, seeking) behind my attempt to accept. I secretly believed that if I accepted the pain, *it would go away*. My *rejection* of pain was disguised as acceptance! What an ingenious place for the seeker to hide—right at the heart of a beautiful spiritual practice! Accepting done with any kind of hope, motive, or expectation is not real acceptance—it is rejection in disguise.

What I didn't realize back then was the unconditional, all-encompassing nature of this deep acceptance. I was so busy *trying* to accept that I ended up missing this deep acceptance of life—in which even my failure to accept was accepted! Yes, this is how radical this acceptance is: even your nonacceptance of pain is allowed into what you are. All waves are accepted by the ocean, and if what's happening right now is nonacceptance of pain, then that is accepted too. The pain is okay, and your dislike of pain, your wanting to be free from it, is okay. The seeker is accepted even in their failure to accept.

And clearly, here is a paradox. If my nonacceptance of pain is accepted by life, totally accepted, *then it is no longer nonacceptance*. The nonacceptance transmutes. Logically, philosophically, rationally, this makes no sense, but it is so. But I don't want you to believe me. I want you to discover this truth for yourself. Everything in this book is about that discovery.

This book is about recognizing a deeper sense of okayness, even when on the surface things are not okay. It is about seeing a deeper completeness, even when on the surface things don't seem complete. What I'm talking about is the ultimate relaxation, the ultimate peace, the ultimate rest. It's not about you, a separate person, being relaxed or peaceful, or trying to rest; it's about a deeper sense of relaxation that comes with *knowing* that every thought, every sensation, every feeling, including all the painful ones, are already accepted in the space that you are. Knowing that, in the moment, even your nonacceptance is deeply accepted is something that can crack even the most hardened suffering at its core. You could say perhaps that *all* suffering is simply our blindness to this deepest acceptance.

Viewed from this new perspective, *all suffering is an invitation to deep acceptance of the present moment.* Suffering or stress or psychological discomfort is no longer something bad or evil to be transcended or destroyed; it is a unique opportunity to see what you are still at war with, what you are still seeking. Within suffering, you will always find this war; you will always find blindness to this deepest acceptance. So the war is always an invitation *back* to this deepest acceptance. Suffering hurts, and the hurt points us home.

Nostalgia is a very beautiful word in the English language, and it literally means "the pain of coming home." But it could also mean "the discovery of home, even in the midst of pain," because home is always present, even in the midst of all of those experiences you'd rather escape, just as the ocean is always present, in and as every wave.

We try to cultivate in ourselves qualities such as love, peace, acceptance, and nonattachment. We exhaust ourselves *trying* to love, *trying* to accept, *trying* to relax, *trying* to be nonjudgmental and non-identified, and even *trying* to stop seeking once and for all. But in discovering who we really are, we come to recognize that these qualities are not the result of the effort of a separate person, but are naturally present in who we are before we identify ourselves as a separate person. Who we are is *naturally* loving, accepting, deeply relaxed, and always at peace, never attached to any form, and who we are has never been seeking anything. It is naturally nonjudgmental, choiceless, and always free from identification. It is the ocean, always at rest even amidst the storm of life, forever deeply allowing every wave without judgment, resistance, or attachment. The end of the search of a lifetime is not a future goal, but who we already are.

What does life look like when viewed from this place of deep acceptance, this place of ever-present completeness? What does life look like when you recognize yourself not as a separate person, not as a separate and incomplete wave in a vast ocean, seeking home, but as the ocean itself, already complete, already home, no matter what is happening? What does life look like when you know yourself to be the wide-open space of acceptance, in which all thoughts, all sensations, all feelings, all waves of experience are deeply allowed to come and go?

And in recognizing yourself as this vast ocean, what then is your relationship to the waves? Are they separate from what you are, or are you now intimate with every single one of them?

An Exploration of
Present-Moment Awareness

The most useful piece of learning . . . is to unlearn what is untrue.
ANTISTHENES

It's now time to challenge some of our most basic assumptions about reality.

Take a moment now. Come right back to present experience, to what's actually happening where you are. See, hear, look freshly at your own experience. Begin again, as if you were a child seeing the world for the first time—because you're *always* seeing it for the first time. In this moment, life is always new. You have never experienced this moment before and never will again. The sounds of this moment have never been heard before. This moment's feelings have never been felt before. These words have never been read before. And even if you believe that they have, that is a memory, a thought about the past, appearing now, in this fresh, new moment.

When you come right back to what's happening now, what you find is simply the spontaneous play of life. Life is a dance of thoughts, sounds, sensations, smells, all appearing and disappearing freshly and freely in the space that you are. And notice how *effortless* it is to see, to hear, to feel.

Listen—without you having to do anything, sounds simply appear. The sound of breathing, the sound of cars beeping their horns, the television blaring, a bird singing—all of these sounds simply appear and are heard, effortlessly. Close your eyes if you wish, and notice the sheer effortlessness of hearing. You don't even have to remind yourself to hear; you don't have to tell your ears to "do hearing." Hearing just happens, very naturally and effortlessly. You could say that hearing happens without you being involved at all.

And then a thought appears: "I am hearing." What does that mean? It means "I am a separate person, hearing these sounds. There's me, and there are the sounds. I am the subject, and the sounds are the objects. There is a perceiver separate from that which is perceived. The sound is out there, and I am in here."

Thought makes huge assumptions about reality. And we very rarely stop and check these assumptions, to see if they hold up against simple investigation.

"I hear the sounds." Is that really true?

We are now questioning our most basic assumptions about our perception of the world, assumptions that may have been there since we were very young. But, as Jesus said, we must become like little children in order to enter the kingdom of heaven (which is the kingdom of the present moment). So let's explore.

"I hear the sounds." Are there really *two* things—the sound *and* the you who hears it? Does this separation—between the sound and the one who is hearing the sound—ever actually take place? In reality—in direct, unfiltered experience—is there any evidence that there is a separate somebody here, hearing sounds? Is there, in reality, an *I* hearing the sounds, or is hearing simply happening, effortlessly?

Check for yourself. In your direct experience, right now, can you find *two* things—the one who hears the sound *and* the sound itself? Or is there just one thing—the effortless hearing? Can you find any dividing line at all, in time or in space, in your direct experience, between the hearing of the sound and the sound itself? Can you find the one who hears the sound *over here,* separate from the sound *over there?* Or are over here and over there never actually part of your direct experience?

For most of my life, I lived with the assumption that there was a separate me here, a separate self here right at the heart of experience, an entity doing hearing, doing seeing, doing thinking. And yet, upon investigation, that untested theory crumbled. There is nobody here doing the living; there is just life appearing, just the various waves of experience arising and falling, and nobody here at the center of it all.

Again, I don't want you to believe this, but to look for yourself. Can you find the one who hears, the one who sees, the one who thinks? Or is the reality much, much simpler—that sounds appear, seeing happens, thoughts arise—and it's simply another thought that says, "I'm doing that!"

Check for yourself. Which is more true: "Sounds simply appear" or "I hear sounds"? Which statement holds up upon direct investigation? Ponder this question. Meditate on it.

Still, the thought "I hear the sound" or "I think the thought" is allowed to arise; it's simply another wave that is deeply allowed in the ocean of you. And even though ultimately these thoughts are not true, speaking in this way is useful for human communication. In the world in which we live, telling an ear doctor "There are simply sounds appearing, but I cannot find anybody here hearing them" would not be particularly useful—and it would probably result in the speaker being sent to a very different kind of doctor!

And so the thought "I hear" is allowed to arise. But the mystery of existence is that hearing still happens without the thought "I hear," doesn't it? The thought "I hear" doesn't itself hear anything, does it? Without the thought "I see," seeing still happens, doesn't it? Without the thought "I think," thoughts still appear, don't they? Reality is always prior to thought. Thought always comes afterwards, desperately trying to capture a reality that is unlimited, unified, whole, complete, and turn it into a *story* about reality that is always limited, divisive, dualistic, and incomplete. Thought takes effortless hearing and says, "I hear." It takes effortless seeing and says, "I see." It takes effortless living and says, "This is my life!" It's almost as if thought is trying to claim ownership of life. Thought says, "I did that! I made that happen!" Thought wants to take credit for everything. It wants to be in control. It wants to be God.

Young children still have a sense of the mystery at the heart of experience. A woman once told me how one day her young daughter ran up to her, clutching some paintings she'd been feverishly working on for hours and exclaimed with amazement, "Mummy, Mummy, look what my hands made!" Not, "Look what I made! Aren't I a great artist?" but, "Look what my hands did all by themselves! Isn't that amazing!" The girl was not yet lost in thought-constructed roles; she was not yet identified as being an artist. There was a simple wonder at how life could happen all by itself. Her creativity came out of nowhere; in truth, it was not hers. It belonged to the universe, not to a separate "artist." All honest artists will admit this.

The truth is that we are not the *doers* of life. Life moves in its own way, and it's only afterwards that thought takes credit for things it never did. Thought says, "I did that! I made that happen! I'm in control of life!" and we believe that story until the day we die.

So we say, "I see a tree," and that statement begs the question, *who* is it that sees the tree? Are there *two* things: me and life? The tree *and* the one who sees it? Or is there only the one seamless, unspeakable, unified reality that is life itself, a reality that I cannot in any way separate myself from? In coming back to present experience, all I can find is an effortless seeing that's happening right now, with no division between the one who sees and everything that's being seen. Life has no boundaries. Seeing has no inside or outside. There is simply seeing, simply shapes, colors, and textures appearing in the vast open awareness that I am. I simply cannot find the dividing line between who I am and everything that appears. I cannot find the place where I end and life begins. Maybe the line doesn't exist and never did.

It's only later that thought says, "I. I see. I see . . . a tree." Now there appear to be two things—me and the tree. Now I feel separate from the tree in some inexplicable way; it seems that the tree is somehow outside of me. On some level, now I feel limited and homesick; I feel separate from the tree and long again for union. I feel separate from the sky and long for union. I feel separate from my body and long for union. I feel separate from you and long for union. But prior to thought, prior to the dream of inside and outside, is there really anything to separate us? Is there not just *intimacy?* Is reunion necessary when there is already union?

Prior to thought, *who* is separate from life? *Who* is incomplete? *Who* longs for union?

Jesus once said, "You have to lose your life to save it." That statement always puzzled me—it seems like the ultimate paradox—until I realized that perhaps he was pointing to the total intimacy between what I am, in my essence, and life itself. Yes, in the place where I would expect to find a separate, solid entity called "me," all I can really find is this amazing dance of waves, and nothing to separate myself from them. In the absence of me, I find the presence of the world. The world and I are in love—in the true meaning of the word *love.* I lose identification with "my life" and discover my inseparability from life itself. I discover that I am not some disembodied awareness or consciousness or soul or spirit detached from life, floating above or beyond or behind life, or existing before or after life. I *am* life itself.

Present experience is so full of sights and sounds and smells and sensations that there is no room left for a separate me. Life squeezes me out!

The spiritual teacher Nisargadatta Maharaj made this beautiful statement: "Wisdom says I am *nothing*. Love says I am *everything*. Between the two my life flows." As the vast ocean of Being, you are no thing in particular. You are not a me or a you. What you are is the vast open space in which everything happens, and the recognition of that brings clarity and wisdom. But clarity and wisdom are not complete without their reflection: love. And love comes from the recognition that, as open space, as the ocean, what you are unconditionally and deeply *accepts* all the waves that appear—all the sights and sounds and smells and sensations that are appearing now. Everything is inseparable from the nothing that you are. In your eyes, everything is beloved. The recognition of wisdom is truly incomplete without the recognition of love.

I find that many spiritual seekers get stuck in the "nothing" aspect of realization and are left with only an intellectual understanding of awakening, which does not bring total freedom and rest. The true end of suffering comes from the recognition of this total intimacy with life itself—in other words, the deep acceptance of "everything" appearing in experience. In this deep acceptance, mind and heart are one. Nothing *is* everything; they were never two separate things. Mental clarity and certainty give way to deep acceptance of this moment. And there, the war ends.

Yes, right at the heart of our experience we find an intimacy, a total inseparability of all the waves of experience— thoughts, sounds, smells, feelings, sensations. These waves are not separate things that come and go within us or things that come from outside of us and move through us. They *are* us.

This intimacy is what we are all looking for, in a million different ways. It is the perfect inseparability of absolute and relative, yin and yang, masculine and feminine, nothing and everything, clarity and love, humanity and divinity, and it is right here, in something as simple as seeing a tree, hearing a bird singing, or feeling intense pain. And yet we look for it "out there," in the world of time and space, in other people, in far-off places, in other realms, in the beyond. But if we listen very carefully, life is always calling us back *here,* to where we already are, to our true home beyond words, to the true beyond.

"IT'S ALL IN YOUR MIND"

There's an idea common in spiritual teachings and espoused by some scientists and philosophers, that the world exists only in our minds or in our brains—that the world is merely our imagination or even worse, that it is just a mistake of perception. But is this ever part of your direct experience of life? Do you experience the world as *inside* something else, something called a mind? Where exactly is this mind that the world is supposed to be in? And *whose* mind is it? Mine? What is "mine" in direct experience?

When I take a fresh look, right now, again what I find is that thoughts appear, smells appear, sounds appear, feelings appear—all in the open space that I am—but there is no evidence that they appear *in* something else called a mind. I can't find any evidence that something called a mind is producing all that is thought, seen, smelled, heard, or felt. I can't find any evidence that these waves of experience come from a mind or come from anything or anywhere else. I just can't find any mind—none outside of thought arising at present. Thought says, "There is a separate mind," but that's just a thought appearing. When I was a child, I learned that I "have" a mind. But is it true?

All I ever find, when I look, is *present* experience. I do not find past or future, I find *now*—and if I do find past and future, they appear as memories and ideas appearing now. It's all now.

And what I find now is that experience is not inside or outside of me. I simply don't find any inside or outside here. There is just total intimacy with all that appears. Experience is not contained within anything, nor can I find any evidence that it is outside of anything.

And so my experience of the room I'm sitting in is not "in my mind"; I don't find any evidence for that. My experience of the room is right here, *as* the room. It is not separate from the room. It *is* the room, as it's being perceived. Experience has no location; it's not located in the head or in the brain. It is everywhere, just as the ocean is present in all of its waves. It is the mug of tea I'm drinking. It is the sky and the stars. It is the leaves crunching beneath my feet as I walk to the post office. The world is not "out there," nor is it "in my mind." It is intimate with what I am. It follows me everywhere. I cannot shake it off. I don't enter and leave the world; the world is always right here. I don't move through the world; it moves with me. And there is no me separate from it. (Oh, don't you love words!)

Similarly, my experience of the sun is not in my brain, my head, or my mind. I never experience it as being inside me in any way. My experience of the sun is not located inside something else. The sun is simply *here*, in present experience. I cannot say the sun is inside me, and I cannot say it is outside of me either.

Now, conventional wisdom tells us that the sun is a giant ball of burning gas millions of miles away from our physical bodies. And that is true, relatively speaking; let's not deny it. But what is also true—and this is the real miracle—is that the sun is always right *here*, in the intimacy of present experience. It appears in the intimacy that I am. It is the warmth on my face. It is the heat on my skin. It is the glare in my eyes. It is a dear, old, familiar, and close friend, who has been with me for as long as I can remember. It is not far away from who I really am. It is *here*.

Although from one perspective, a wave may seem far from another wave in the ocean, from the perspective of the ocean, since every wave is the ocean itself, the concept of distance, or lack of it, becomes meaningless. The ocean has no specific location—which is to say, it is in all locations at once. In other words, it is always *here*.

All waves in the ocean that I am are essentially myself, even if they appear to be millions of miles away.

THE STORY OF THE WORLD

You can experience something in your world—a car, a tree, pain, frustration, a cheese sandwich, the sun, a spoon—only if on some level you *tell yourself* what you are experiencing. In order to experience anything, you must have a *thought story* about what that thing is. Otherwise, you have no way of *knowing* what you are experiencing. Without the story, you really have no way of knowing what you are looking at. Thought labels everything that appears. How do you *know* you are looking at the sun unless thought tells you it is the sun? How do you know what you're eating is a cheese sandwich unless you have the story "This Is a Cheese Sandwich"? How do you know that a bird is a bird without all of those ideas, concepts, beliefs, and memories that tell you it's a bird? How can you know the names of the available dishes at the restaurant of life without first consulting thought's menu?

Now, some people have taken this message too far. They say that without thought, there is *nothing*. This is a misconception because "nothing" is just another thought—the opposite of something. Reality is beyond even that. Without the thought story telling you what you are experiencing, it's not that there is something called "nothing"—it's that there is no way of *knowing* what you are experiencing. There is utter not-knowing. You meet the world for the first time. You are in the Garden of Eden, and nothing has been named yet. This is beyond all our ideas of *something* and *nothing*.

In order to experience *anything*—in other words, in order to know what you are experiencing—on some level you must *tell yourself* what you are experiencing. In order to experience a chair, for example, you must on some level tell yourself that it's a chair. You must have a chair story running; otherwise you have no way of knowing what it is. The thought "chair" appears, and suddenly I know I'm experiencing a chair. I have learned about chairs. I have sat on many chairs in the past. Perhaps I have read the history of chairs. I know what chairs are; therefore, I know that I'm experiencing a chair. Without that thought, can I *know* what I'm experiencing? Without thought, can there be a knowable world?

Watch babies explore their environment. They have not yet learned the names for things. They have not yet learned the value of things. Cheap and expensive, useful and useless, sacred and profane mean nothing to them. You hand them a worthless piece of plastic, and they are fascinated. You hand them a priceless diamond ring, and they are fascinated. And when they are no longer fascinated, they move onto the next object. They have no fixed story yet about the world. They are meeting everything for the first time and exploring. They are smelling, touching, tasting, wondering about everything. Quite literally, they exist in wonder.

Before we name the world, there is only mystery.

At some point in a child's life, we tell them, "That's a chair." Now they know what it is. It's an "object" called "a chair." It's separate from what they are. They no longer have to explore it, to run their fingers over it, to look at it up close. They no longer need to be fascinated by it, to be intimate with it. It's now a useful piece of information, a "fact," rather than a mystery to be explored. For the rest of their lives, they will look at a chair and tell themselves that they *know* what it is. But do they really know what it is? Beyond the words, isn't there just mystery? Isn't there *still* wonder and not-knowing?

In order to experience your mother, father, sister, or brother, on some level, you must tell yourself (or remind yourself) who they are. Without *your story* about who they are, you have no way of knowing who they are, do you? Without your story, you meet them, quite literally, for the very first time. Without the story, there is only total intimacy. Beyond the story, there is love. Love means "not two."

However, we *forget* that we are experiencing our own *stories* about the world—our own thoughts, our own labels, our own interpretations, our own memories, our own prejudices, our own fears, our own conditioning, our own dreams. And we fall into the belief that there *is* actually a separate world out there, with separate objects and people, and that we are experiencing this world objectively and reporting back on it. We forget that we are experiencing a projection of our own dream, and we live as if we are separate from—and slaves to and victims of—a world "out there." We forget the total intimacy right at the heart of life, and we fall into a world of separation and fragmentation, a world where I'm over here, and everything else is over there, and we are forever at a distance. This forgetting is the origin of all loneliness, isolation, and depression.

Then we start talking about things like "my mind" as if it were a real thing, a substance, an entity, in our world. We forget who we really are—the open space that holds all form—and we identify ourselves as being separate minds and bodies, separate people in our separate worlds. Fragmentation and isolation result. And then, in our fragmented state, we turn to religion and to spirituality to set ourselves free from fragmentation. And we do all of this because we don't take the time to really look deeply into our own experience and see the intimate truth.

Think of the freedom that would be unleashed if we taught our children to look—to really look—at their present experience and discover the intimacy present within it. It would shake society to its foundations. Maybe that's why we don't do it.

THE STORY OF MYSELF

Not only do you not have an inside and an outside, but you also never actually experience yourself directly as a person. (Try telling this to a psychiatrist!) All you ever find are thoughts appearing, sounds appearing, feelings appearing in what you are. And then thought says, "These are *my* thoughts, *my* feelings, *my* emotions. Life is happening to *me*." That's where the story of the person begins: in identification with the forms that pass through awareness, identification with thoughts and feelings, identification with the waves that appear and disappear in the ocean that is you.

Find a photograph of yourself as a child. Who is that in the photograph? You may reply, "That's me." But that answer begs the question, what is this "me" that you are claiming to be? Is the me in the photograph the same me that's here now?

The thoughts, feelings, beliefs, and ideas that are appearing and disappearing in your experience right now are certainly not the same ones that were appearing and disappearing all of those years ago. Your story about yourself has changed since then, maybe beyond all recognition. Back then you wanted to be a fireman or a ballet dancer. Back then you were terrified of the monster in the closet, and you believed that tiny pink dinosaurs lived underground in your neighbor's back garden.

These days your priorities have changed. You no longer worry about the monster in the closet. You worry about making enough money to put your kids through school. You worry about your pension, about the stock market, about the war, about the latest terrorist scare, about not becoming enlightened in this lifetime. Can you really say that you are the same "me" now that you were then? Your physical appearance has changed totally; in fact, there is not a single cell in your body that remains from that me. Your face, your voice, your hair—everything has changed.

But you still somehow still feel like you, in a way that you can't explain. There is a certain sense of *being here* that hasn't changed. The sense of "I am" has remained constant. The ocean has remained; it's just the waves that have moved. Millions of thoughts have come and gone. All kinds of feelings have appeared and disappeared. But this basic feeling of Being has remained. And yet, we can't really talk about what that Being is. It feels somehow intimate—somehow totally yourself, and yet somehow unknowable, somehow beyond you.

Take a moment now to gently turn your attention to what it actually feels like to be you. By "you," I don't mean the thoughts and judgments about yourself that come and go or the sensations and emotions that arise and fall throughout the day. I don't mean the images and pictures of your past or the worries about your uncertain future. I am pointing to something that comes before all of that. I am pointing to the sense of just being you, simply you, here and now, a sense that has been here since you were a child. It is a very subtle but very alive feeling of presence that has never gone away, no matter what you've achieved, no matter what you've lost, no matter how many spiritual insights or experiences you've had. I'm not talking about "you" as a special state or experience. I am not talking about a higher self, or an awakened self, or a special version of the self, but the simple and very ordinary feeling of being you, in this moment. You don't even have to understand what I'm talking about in order to know this basic sense of me-ness. Whether or not you think you understand, and even if you feel confused and frustrated right now, notice that just behind this struggle, there is still the simple feeling of being you. I'm really pointing to something very, very simple indeed—too simple for the mind to comprehend. You already know who you really are. You are already completely you, no matter what happens. This simple recognition is at the heart of what this book is all about.

It is always strange these days for me to meet up with someone who knew me when I was younger. I feel like I've changed so much over the past few years—so much that I barely recognize the me that I apparently used to be. And yet that old me still seems to exist for other people. I meet old school friends or relatives that I haven't seen since I was a teenager, and it's always amazing to discover how they are still living with an old story of Jeff Foster, based on what they experienced many years ago. Everyone lives with their own version of me. Even if you have changed beyond all recognition—even if you are dead!—people will still be carrying their own story about who you are, based on memory. We live in our stories of each other. Do we ever truly meet each other?

I walk into the room, and you project your story of me onto this body. But if you know the story of my life, the details, the history, do you really know who I am? If you know *about* me, do you really *know* me? If you ask me to tell you about myself, and I answer with a story about what I do for a living, about my relationships, about my successes and failures, my likes and dislikes, am I really telling you the truth of who I am? Or am I just giving you a *story* about who I am, the story of a character in a movie? Does telling you about what I've done in the past and what I hope to do in the future really tell you anything about who is here right now, in this moment? Can the past or future really capture this present moment?

Without referring to the past or future, who are you, right now?

When we talk about ourselves, what we are usually talking about is the *story* of ourselves: "I am good. I am bad. I am successful. I am a failure. I am kind. I am strong. I am intelligent. I am black, white, short, tall, handsome, beautiful, rich, poor. I am Jewish. I am Christian. I am a Buddhist. I am a lawyer, a shopkeeper, a doctor, a politician, an artist. I am shy. I am extroverted. I am spiritual. I am musical. I am sporty. I am enlightened. I am unenlightened." And so on.

But as open space, all the stories in the world cannot touch what I am. As open space, I am what I am right now, in this moment, and nothing more. I am not what I have been or was or will be. As open space, I am not the story of a person in time. I am not the image of a person in a world. I am not an incomplete seeker looking for something in the future to complete myself. I am what's appearing now.

We talk about finding our "true identity," but our true identity does not lie in the *story* of our lives. I am not the story of my achievements or my failures. I am not the story of my social status. I am not the story of my wealth or poverty. I am not the story of my successful or failed relationships. I am not the story of my illness or disability. I am not the story of my childhood or my past or future lives. I am not the story of my race, my color, my religion. I am not the story of my beliefs. I am not the story of my search for enlightenment or my success or failure to find it.

I am simply what's happening in this moment. That is where my identity truly lies—in the here and now, not in the time-bound story of me. I am *identical* with this moment.

That is the true meaning of the word *identity:* "to be identical with." What I am is *identical* with life as it appears now, just as the ocean is always identical with its waves.

In Shakespeare's *King Lear,* there is a famous scene in which the once-great king wanders naked on a heath during a terrible storm; the wind howls and the rain lashes his frail body. The awesome power of nature shocks him into a realization of his total insignificance in the face of life. He is forced to see the bigger picture: He is not really a king at all. He is a frail, vulnerable, and mortal human being, ultimately powerless to control the universe. He had simply been playing the *role* of a king—and he had *forgotten* that he was playing it. He had been living with a false image of himself. "King Lear" was simply a temporary shape that consciousness had taken on in him; it was not who he really was, in his essence. Stripped of his kingly role—his costume, his castle, his power—stripped of all images, lashed by the storm, who was he, in *this* moment? Who was King Lear, without his image of "King Lear"?

It's no wonder that scene is so powerful—it touches something profound and essential about the human condition. Underneath our roles—as kings, queens, mothers, fathers, sisters, brothers, wives, husbands, homeless people, doctors, lawyers, therapists, shopkeepers, dancers, artists, spiritual seekers, spiritual teachers—who are we, really? As individual waves in the ocean of life, we all may be different in shape, size, color, beliefs, backgrounds, experiences, knowledge, skills, but are we not all equally *water?* We may differ in *appearance,* we may each be unique expressions of the ocean, but our *essence* is the same. Is a king really any more powerful, in the true meaning of the word, than his court jester?

Underneath all our roles, underneath all the images of ourselves, even if we are kings and queens, saints or sinners, are we not all simply this intimate open space of awareness? Are we not all simply identical with this moment?

As open space, in fact, it's very hard to talk about myself at all. It's very hard to tell a story about a fixed identity, for I notice that here, in the open space of awareness, everything is constantly changing. Thoughts appear and disappear. Feelings appear and disappear. All kinds of sensations and sounds and smells and tastes come and go. Here, everything is alive, always moving. I would have to press pause on this ever-changing landscape in order to begin to tell a fixed story about myself. I would need to somehow freeze the river of life, fix this moment, point to it, and say, "This feeling, this thought—that's me!" But the beauty of life is that it cannot be frozen or fixed. It's always moving; it's always dancing. The river of life cannot be stopped by anyone.

It's no wonder that the word *moment* and the word *movement* come from the same root (the Latin word *movere*, which means "to move"). This moment is inseparable from the movement of life. Stillness is in love with movement. The ocean is in love with its waves.

Hopefully we are now in a position to clearly understand what the spiritual teachings are talking about when they use the phrase "There is no me" or "There is no self." Look into present experience, and what you will discover is that there is no separate, independent thing called a self in this open space that you are. There is only the dance of life, the dance of waves—thoughts, sensations, feelings, all appearing and disappearing, all moving through. And ultimately the thought "There is no self" is just another thought, another viewpoint, that appears and disappears. It is another wave that comes and goes like any other wave. Even the thought "There is no me" cannot define what I am!

The thought "There is no self" can actually be very misleading, if you do not clearly see what those words are pointing to. If you're not careful, you simply start to *believe* that there is no self. "There is no self" becomes your new religion, your new image of yourself! A self starts to believe that there is no self. A wave, still experiencing itself as a separate wave, still suffering and still longing for rest, tells itself "There is no wave." The seeker is ingenious, isn't it?

I remember, some years ago, when I saw myself as a very serious spiritual seeker, one day my brother asked me to do the dishes, and I, in all seriousness, replied that there was "nobody here to do the dishes." I told him that if he believed that the dishes needed cleaning then he was still stuck in duality and delusion. Back then I was very much stuck in spiritual concepts. Nonduality had become my new religion, although I believed I had freed myself from all religion. I thought I had found the truth of all existence. I was nobody; I had lost my self, and I was living in a world full of annoying somebodies who didn't recognize who I really was and, even worse, wanted me to do the dishes for them! But now, looking back, I see my own arrogance—and my own innocence too, of course. I think secretly I just wanted to get out of having to do the dishes, and I was using spiritual concepts to avoid authentic human engagement.

Something else that seems to cause confusion among spiritual seekers is the idea that the self is an illusion. I may be an illusion, but when I bang my head accidentally as I get out of a car, it damn well hurts! Or as Neil Young sang, "Though my problems are meaningless, that don't make 'em go away."

It might help to look at what the word *illusion* actually means. It derives from the Latin word *illudere*, which means "to mock at" or literally "to play with" (from *in*, meaning "at," plus *ludere*, meaning "to play"). So the word *illusion* simply means "a play" or "a deceptive appearance." It doesn't mean "nonexistence." This understanding can help us clear up much confusion. The self, the me, is an illusion, *not because it doesn't exist, but because it doesn't exist in the way we imagine it*. We *imagine* that there is a solid and separate me—a separate entity here at the center of life, an entity that is in charge of life—but upon investigation, that assumption crumbles. The illusion is seen through: what I really am is intimate with life itself. It's not that the wave doesn't exist—it's that the wave is inseparable from the ocean.

The separation of the "I" (or ego) from life itself is the illusion, but I, as a unique, unparalleled, never-to-be-repeated expression of that ocean, still appears *to exist.* "We are one, but we're not the same," as Bono sings in U2's beautiful song "One."

There is no wholeness without the appearance of diversity. Wholeness actually expresses itself as the astonishing diversity and multiplicity of life.

And so it's not that there is no me—it's that when I take a fresh look, right now, I can't find something *separate* from life itself called a me. I can't find anything here that's solid and enduring in time and space. I can't find anything divided from this moment. I find only passing forms—waves of experience appearing and disappearing. I find only thoughts, memories, images, sounds, sensations, smells, feelings—all coming and going in the space that I am. The story of me is something else that comes and goes in the space that I am. "I" come and go in what I am!

The illusion is that there is something solid, fixed, separate here. In the end, I can say, "There is no fixed self." Or actually, I could say that "everything is Self"—all the waves are inseparable from what I am. *The words you use cease to matter when you really see what's going on.* All the words in the world just dissolve back into the space, into the silence.

THE DIFFERENCE BETWEEN FEELING AND BEING

As the open space in which all waves appear, you cannot actually be *defined* by any of the waves that appear. Anger, fear, sadness, boredom, joy—these waves simply appear and disappear in what you are. You are intimate with them, *but they cannot define you.* The happiest feelings, the saddest feelings, the most painful feelings, the most intense feelings, every kind of thought, no matter how strange, unpleasant, or "abnormal," can all come and go in what you are. And what you are remains untouched, in the same way that no matter what is projected onto a movie screen, the screen remains pristine.

What you are is simply the *capacity* to think anything and to *feel* anything, but you are not defined by any of the thoughts and feelings that appear. What you are is like a sieve through which all human experience can pass. You are the movie screen that no movie can ever stick to.

Anger can come and go in what you are, but there is no angry *person*. There is fear, but no fearful *person*. There is sadness, but no sad *person* anywhere to be found. You are not a limited person—you are unlimited and unbounded capacity for all of life.

To understand what it means to be the capacity for every wave, it is important to understand the difference between *feeling* something and *being* something. You can *feel* ugly (or weak or hopeless or confused or fearful or bored or excited— whatever) in the moment, but in reality, who you really are cannot *be* that. You can *feel* ugly, but, as open space, you cannot *be* ugly. There is no ugly *person*. The ugly feeling cannot *define* you. The open space that you are is beyond all of the opposites. Feelings of both ugliness *and* beauty appear in what you are, and what you are remains untouched by either polarity. What you are is not made less complete by feelings of ugliness, nor is it made more complete by feelings of beauty. What you are is neither ugly nor beautiful; it *allows* both ugliness and beauty, but cannot be *defined* by either, just as the ocean *allows* all of its waves, but cannot be *defined* by any particular wave that appears.

So you cannot *be* ugly, but you can *feel* ugly. There is no ugly person, just present-moment feelings of ugliness appearing in you. You cannot *be* a failure, but you can *feel* like a failure. There is no failed person, just feelings of failure appearing and disappearing in what you are. You cannot *be* helpless, but you can *feel* helpless. There is no helpless person, just feelings of helplessness coming and going in you. You cannot *be* anything in particular (because what you are holds every feeling as it comes and goes), but you can *feel* anything and everything. All feelings—any feeling that a human being is capable of, any feeling that any human being has ever had—are allowed to come and go in what you are. All of human consciousness, in that sense, is available to you. Anything that you can feel, I can feel. Anything that you can think, I can think. There is no wave that is alien to the ocean of consciousness. There is no thought, no feeling, in reality, that is alien to what you are. You are the space that holds all of humanity. You allow the entire river of human consciousness to flow through you. You are the no-thing that holds *everything* as it flows through. In the absence of a separate person, you discover all of humanity.

Much of our suffering rests on the assumption that if we *feel* something for too long or too intensely, or at all, we will *become* it. We assume that if we really allow the feeling to be there, it will stick and end up defining us. Much of our suffering rests on what amounts to superstition! Just because you feel like a failure does not mean that you are a failure. Just because you feel ugly does not mean that you are ugly. Just because you feel a wave, it does not mean that the wave can define you.

In our drive to define ourselves, to distinguish ourselves from others, to hold up a consistent story about who we are, what we end up doing is not allowing in feelings that conflict with the image or story of ourselves that we are trying to hold up. We say, "This feeling is me" or "This feeling is not me." If I see myself as a beautiful, attractive person, I am *not* going to allow an ugly wave in. I can't allow myself to feel ugly. That wave just doesn't fit with how I want to see myself and how I want you to see me. If I feel ugly, I start to feel that there's something wrong—that I don't "feel myself" today. Or if I have an idea of myself as a successful person, I am not going to allow a failure wave in. It doesn't fit with my idea of myself. I cannot allow myself to feel failure. If I see myself as a strong person and want others to see me as a strong person, I cannot allow myself to feel weak. I cannot allow any wave into my experience that threatens my idea of myself.

If we were actually in control of the waves that appear, we would simply be able to shut out all the waves that don't support our story of ourselves. But, ultimately, we are not in control of the ocean of life. Despite our best efforts, thoughts and feelings that we do not want keep on appearing. We try to banish the ugly, fearful, painful, uncomfortable waves; the failure waves; the weakness waves; the "negative energy" waves; the "dark" waves, and we find that, ultimately, it's not possible. They appear anyway. We cannot shut out half of the ocean. The ocean of life is wild and free and cannot be tamed or repressed.

Why can we not control the waves? Why do our unwanted waves appear? Because in the world of duality, the opposites *must* appear together. This truth is very important to understand too. Our experience is in perfect balance. If there is *beautiful,* there must be *ugly.* If there is *success,* there must be *failure.* If there is *enlightened,* there must be *unenlightened.* If there is *loved,* there must be *unloved.* This is the way things are, and it's not a problem until we go to war with the way things are, until we go against the balance of life.

The beauty of life is that it's constantly changing, moving. We cannot feel the same thing *all* the time. In present experience, there is no "all the time," and there is also no "never." There is only the dance of waves *now.* When we say, "I want to *be* attractive. I want to *be* beautiful," what we must mean is that we want to *feel* attractive all the time and never feel ugly. Remember, what you are cannot *be* anything in particular, but what you are is the capacity to *feel* anything now. We want to be something fixed and solid in time and space, and yet when we look, we find that our feelings are constantly moving, changing, in the timeless moment.

The reality is that, in any moment, we can feel beautiful, or we can feel ugly. Sometimes we feel like a success; sometimes we feel like a failure. Sometimes we feel weak; sometimes we feel strong. Sometimes we feel certain; sometimes we feel uncertain. Sometimes we feel joyful; sometimes we feel sad. Sometimes we feel in favor of something; sometimes we feel against that same thing. This is the way things are, and it is totally natural to feel these seemingly contradictory feelings one after the other or even to feel them at the same time. We don't like paradox, but when you understand that we are essentially paradoxical creatures *and that is deeply okay*, you see how natural it is to *not* feel the same thing all the time!

In the ocean that is you, change, flux, and inconsistency are the way of things. The changeless ocean loves to express itself as waves that constantly move. But in our quest to be a consistent self, to have a fixed, consistent, and changeless story of who we are, we label inconsistency as negative and try to avoid it at all costs. We want to feel the same tomorrow as we do today. We want to think the same thoughts, have the same opinions, want the same things, believe the same beliefs, day after day, year after year. We don't want to flip-flop. We don't want to be seen as flaky, changeable, unreliable, unable to make up our minds. Change, movement, flow are the way of things, and yet we want to be *fixed*. We want to hold up a fixed *image* of who we are, to tell a consistent story about ourselves from day to day. We want to be *something*, and yet our nature prevents us from ever being a fixed "thing." Because of our misunderstanding of who we really are, we go to war with the wholeness of experience, trying to freeze the natural flow of life—and much frustration and suffering result.

We are at war with the opposites; we reject any opposite that doesn't match our image of ourselves, and we don't realize something very important: *in reality, there are no opposites.* Opposites are a creation of the mind. Only the mind splits reality, splits experiences into two and then seeks one of the opposites and tries to escape the other.

Here's something that's crucial to understand: *In reality, feelings have no opposite. Energy in the body has no opposite. Life itself has no opposite.*

Does the sound of a bird singing have an opposite? In this moment, listening to the bird singing, is there such thing as an opposite? Thought might say, "The opposite of the bird singing is the bird *not* singing," but that is just another thought, another image, appearing right now. Does the actual *tweet-tweet* of the bird—listen to it now—have an opposite, in reality?

Does this moment have an opposite? Does the presence of life here and now have an opposite? Does anything actually oppose it?

Does a sensation have an opposite? Pinch yourself now. Bring awareness to the intense sensations that result. Can you find an opposite to these sensations? Yes, thought would say, "The opposite of this pain is the absence of this pain," but again, that's just another thought appearing now. In reality, does present sensation have an opposite that you can actually find in present experience?

Is an ugly feeling the opposite of a beautiful feeling? Or are they two very different experiences, with different sensations, different tastes? Is a happy feeling the opposite of a sad feeling? Thought would say they are opposites, but outside of thought, can you find an opposite?

In reality, there is no such thing as an opposite of a feeling or emotion. Every feeling and emotion is a complete experience in itself.

Experience itself has no opposite.

Feeling ugly is not the opposite of anything—it's just feeling ugly. Without calling feeling ugly "negative" and feeling beautiful "positive," without making them into opposites, we see that feeling ugly is simply an experience happening now—just a wave of experience, just something passing through. No wave is intrinsically better or worse than any other wave, because no wave is the opposite of any other wave. Every wave is equally water. Feeling ugly is not the opposite of anything—it's just feeling ugly. It's just life-energy moving in a particular way.

And let's go deeper. Not only is beauty not the opposite of ugliness, but ugliness is also simply a concept in itself, and as such, it cannot capture the actual present-moment experience. In other words, without the story that what I am experiencing is ugliness, what is actually happening here?

Without the story that what I am experiencing now is failure, what is actually here?

Without the story that what I am experiencing now is pain, or grief, or boredom, or anger, or discomfort, or depression, or confusion, or even seeking, what is actually here?

Without any story about what is happening now, without labeling this experience as "failure" and comparing it with success, without labeling it "ugliness" and comparing it with beauty, without calling it "anger" or "fear" or "pain" and comparing it with its conceptual opposite, how do I know what it is that I am feeling?

As I was saying before, without the story, you have no way of knowing what you are experiencing. Without any story, without naming the waves, life is simply raw energy moving. It is the ocean—nameless and mysterious. We try to put a label to that energy. We judge it, try to escape it, make it the negative of an opposite positive and then seek the positive.

And yet underneath all of this, we don't really know what we are running away from in the first place. We simply call a wave "fear," "anger," "sadness," "boredom," "grief," "joy," or "pain" because these are the names and concepts we have learned, and then we try to escape these waves or hold onto them. But take away those labels, and what are you really trying to escape from or hold onto? Do you actually know? What happens when we drop all the labels, all the learned descriptions, and face the raw energy of life, as it is in this moment, without trying to change, escape from, or cling to it? What happens when we drop all descriptions of what this moment is or is not and deeply feel into present sensations?

This is where the real adventure of life begins.

When you go beyond the story of what you are feeling, you come to see that *you never really knew what you were running away from.* And you meet the raw energy of life. You stand naked in front of life—and this is true healing. It is the falling away of all ideas of how this moment should be.

It's when we label the waves that the war begins. The moment we label a wave of experience, we set it up as the opposite of another wave, even though, in reality, waves have no opposite. In every label, there is an implicit judgment. In creating the opposites beauty and ugliness and then seeking beauty, we go to war with what we call ugly. In trying to be beautiful, in trying to *feel* beautiful, in trying not to feel ugly, we end up going to war with this present experience and trying to reach its opposite—even though it actually has no opposite! No wonder we suffer. We think, "This feeling of ugliness is a threat to my completeness. If I can get rid of it, if I can move from ugly to beautiful, then I'll be complete." And the game is on.

What images of yourself are you trying to hold up? What do you want to be seen as? Happy, beautiful, successful, peaceful, blissful, enlightened? Expert? Teacher? The one who knows? The one who has worked everything out? What don't you want to be seen as? Sad, stressed, unpopular, ugly, unintelligent, a failure? Which images of yourself are not okay? What do you want to feel? What don't you want to feel? Which waves are not okay in your world?

I once worked with a woman who told me about her lifelong quest to be beautiful. She desperately wanted to be desirable to men. She wanted to be the most beautiful woman in the room. She thought night and day about her looks and spent huge amounts of money on clothes and cosmetics and plastic surgery, all in her search for beauty. After I'd been talking to her for a while, it became clear where this obsession with beauty came from. Secretly, she felt desperately ugly.

For her whole life she had felt ugly, and she was trying to cover up her feelings of ugliness with fashion and makeup and the appearance of beauty. While there's nothing wrong with wanting to be attractive—making efforts to look attractive can be an enjoyable and fun part of life—her seeking wasn't working for her. It wasn't removing the incompleteness at the bottom of it all. Her attempt to be beautiful wasn't removing her feelings of ugliness. In fact, she felt uglier than ever, and she was becoming more desperate than ever to escape her feelings of ugliness.

Whenever she felt the ugliest, she would dress up, go out to a nightclub, find a man, and have superficial, unfulfilling sex with him. And for a while she would feel attractive, beautiful, sexy, and wanted. For a while, she would feel complete. It seemed as though sex had the power to take away her feelings of ugliness. Sex had become her guru.

But the morning after, her feelings of ugliness would return worse than ever, and now they were mixed with guilt, because she knew on some level she was not being authentic; she was not revealing who she really was in the moment. She was pretending to be beautiful, when in fact she felt ugly and could not reveal her feelings. It was all an act, and her act was not providing her with what she truly longed for: love; wholeness; release from her burden of seeking; home; to be loved for who she really was, not for who she was pretending to be. The seeker of love will do anything to feel loved, if only for a short while.

Do you see how her quest for love and beauty in the future was identical with her attempt to escape ugliness in present experience? On some level, feelings of ugliness were a threat to her, to her idea of who she was, to who she wanted to be. Ugliness equaled "not okay." She revealed to me that she was abused as a child, and feeling ugly also brought with it feelings of unworthiness, guilt, and failure. Basically, feeling ugly was linked to feeling unloved and unlovable, so she couldn't allow herself to feel ugly for very long. Going out and having unfulfilling sex was a great way to distract herself from these uncomfortable feelings. But in the end, she always felt uglier than ever, as well as more disconnected, more fake, and more unloved.

It had simply never occurred to her that it could be deeply okay to feel ugly sometimes. Surely *feeling* ugly is a sign of *being* ugly and, therefore, is not okay? She had associated *feeling* ugly with *being* ugly. She believed that only an ugly *person* would feel ugly. This was her superstition.

In seeing that the ugliness wave was already accepted in the ocean—in other words, seeing that even in the midst of the most overwhelming feeling of ugliness, the open space that she was remained unaffected—she could then allow herself to feel ugly and know that, on the deepest level, this feeling was okay. The ugliness could not define her. So although she could *feel* ugly, as the open space of awareness, she could not *be* ugly. Nobody is ugly. We just feel ugly sometimes. And when we are at war with that feeling in ourselves, we project that rejection onto the world and call other people ugly.

The woman came to see that feeling ugly sometimes was not a fault of hers, but a natural part of the total balance of human experience. Lots of people feel ugly, but don't admit it. It's not the sort of thing that beautiful people talk about—or at least not people who want to be seen as beautiful!

Deep down, neither this woman nor we really want to be beautiful; we want to be *whole*. And being whole means being open to all experience. It means knowing yourself as the space in which ugliness and beauty come and go. In a very strange way—and this may sound a little crazy at first—we long to be ugly, because on some level, we know that ugly is the ocean too, and we know that it's only when we allow ourselves to truly feel ugly that we can also feel truly beautiful.

We don't really long to find what we are looking for. We long to discover that we are already what we are looking for, even in the midst of feelings of ugliness, failure, weakness, insecurity, or total devastation. We actually long for all the things we are running away from—ugliness, failure, fear, weakness, insecurity, devastation—because on some level, we know that in these things is where completeness lies. We long to allow everything.

By seeing that her ugliness was already accepted, this woman discovered that she could finally give up trying to be beautiful and instead simply be honest about the fact that she felt ugly sometimes. By seeing that her ugliness was admitted (in other words, already deeply allowed into present experience), she could admit her ugliness! What a relief to admit the truth of this moment, to finally stop pretending to be something that she knew she wasn't! What a relief to no longer have to hold up a false image of herself! What a relief to be *herself* in the true sense of the word—the wide-open ocean of consciousness in which every wave is deeply accepted.

And the strange thing was that by admitting her feelings of ugliness, she no longer felt the need to cover them up by seeking out men and pretending to be beautiful around them.

She no longer felt the need to hide her feelings of ugliness in the way she was doing before, because she no longer felt the need to hold up an identity of herself as beautiful.

Why must we hold up stories about ourselves? Why do we need any story about ourselves? Why can't present experience just be allowed to be as it is, without us pretending it's something that it's not? Why must we live with an image of who we are? Why can't we simply be honest about present experience instead? Why can't we simply admit what is present and discover that what is present is already admitted by what we are?

The woman no longer wanted to be beautiful. She wanted to be honest instead. She wanted to be authentic instead. She just wanted to feel what she felt—no more, no less. Later, she told me that men were now able to connect with her on a much deeper level, because she gave them permission to admit that *they* felt ugly too sometimes! It was a relief for them to meet a woman who understood them on this deeper level, a woman around whom they did not have to perform. How beautiful it is to meet someone who is honest about their feelings of ugliness. How intimate it is to meet someone in their ugliness, to meet beyond the image. How attractive it is to meet someone who is comfortable with feeling unattractive, someone who is not trying to be attractive. What a relief—for everyone—to no longer have to pretend.

"I am ugly" used to be something this woman would never have been able to admit, because that admission would have been the death of her image of herself as a beautiful person. It used to terrify her to think that others might see her as ugly.

But these days she can say, "I am ugly," and those words have a whole different meaning. "I am ugly" does not mean that there is somebody here who is ugly, a separate person with the quality of being ugly rather than beautiful. There is no ugly person, for in truth there is no person at all. "I am ugly" simply means that the feeling of ugliness can be here, in the open space that I am, sometimes. It is allowed to be here, if it shows up.

The words "I am ugly" can be a celebration of life rather than a negative judgment about a separate person. Life appears as everything—beauty, ugliness, and everything in between—and in the open space that I am, it is all allowed to come and go. I contain it all. I hold it all. I embrace it all. I find all of it in myself: *I am beautiful. I am ugly. I am loved. I am unloved. I am a success. I am a failure. I am joyful. I am sad. I am strong. I am weak. I know. I don't know. I am enlightened. I am unenlightened. I am certain. I am uncertain.* When you're no longer at war with the opposites, there is enough room for all of this. All of human consciousness can pass through you. Everything we once called "negativity" is now seen to be part of the celebration of life. All waves are allowed in the ocean. Our ideas about what is negative and what is not are completely released in deep acceptance.

Do you want to be beautiful? Then you have to deeply accept your ugliness, to come to see that it's allowed in what you are. That's the deal. Do you want to be strong? Then you have to be deeply accepting of weakness, to come to see that it's only when you completely allow all feelings of weakness to be there that a real strength emerges—a strength that is not at war with weakness. That's the deal. Do you want to be a success? Then you have to succeed at loving your failure, realizing that even the most complete feeling of failure is allowed in what you are. That's the deal. Do you want to be loved? Then you have to come to deeply accept any feeling of being unloved, here and now. That's where you discover a love with no opposite—a love that cannot be opposed. That's the deal.

I once asked a businessman who was obsessed with success, "What will happen if you fail?"

"I'll lose my money," he said.

"And then what?" I asked.

"I'll lose my house, my car, my family."

"And then what?"

"I'll end up on the streets, homeless, unprotected, vulnerable to life. I'll be an outcast from society. I'll be *unloved and unwanted*."

Here we got to the core of his fear. It wasn't really about loss of success—it was about loss of love, loss of approval, loss of completeness. He had associated success with completeness, and failure with incompleteness. Unsurprisingly, it turned out that as a child, although he had loving parents, he felt—very subtly—that they loved him more when he succeeded, and he felt ever so slightly rejected by them when he failed. To this day, he is playing out the same patterns: "I'm unloved in my failure and loved in my success." His drive for success wasn't really about money; it was about love.

If you drop down through your deepest, darkest fears—the fear of being ugly, the fear of failure, the fear of poverty, the fear of illness—as you approach rock bottom, what you'll nearly always find is the basic fear "I will be unloved." I will be ugly and unloved in that ugliness. I will be in pain and unloved and alone in that pain. I will be incomplete, homesick, and closer to death, in my failure. Our fear is not really the fear of failure or ugliness or pain, but what these things *symbolize* in our world. And for many people, failure is linked to disapproval, rejection, abandonment, and, ultimately, lack of love. Even the most hardheaded businessman is secretly longing for love and running away from the feeling that, in his failure, he is not worthy of love. Not seeing himself as complete here and now, he seeks completeness through success and fears failure.

When you discover who you really are—the wide-open space that holds everything—you discover that failure, illness, ugliness, helplessness, uncertainty, and weakness are there to be embraced, not avoided. All waves—including the ones we fear the most, including the ones that seem most threatening to who we are—are already embraced by life's ocean. What you are is not an image, and it cannot be threatened by any wave. Only an image can be threatened.

Taking your stand as the vast space in which everything happens, and knowing yourself as the capacity for this moment, notice that *all* feelings—good and bad, positive and negative—are already deeply allowed into what you are. They have been appearing all throughout your life, which is all the proof you need. This total embrace of all waves of experience is the love you have always been seeking.

THERE IS NO SUCH THING AS A NEGATIVE THOUGHT

We try so hard to control our thoughts, don't we? We try to have positive, loving, kind, compassionate, spiritual thoughts, and we try to banish bad, evil, destructive, unkind, violent, sinful thoughts. Some thoughts we even call unthinkable. I mustn't think about killing. I mustn't think bad things about those I love. I mustn't have judgments. I mustn't think about sex. I mustn't think about what will happen in the future. I mustn't have negative thoughts. I mustn't have too many thoughts. I mustn't listen to my thoughts. I must be enlightened and free from thought altogether.

Trying to control your thoughts—trying to control the waves in the ocean—is ultimately going to create huge amounts of suffering, because the attempt is based on an illusion about who you are. If you've ever meditated for more than five seconds, you've probably noticed that you're not in control of your thoughts. You can't even know your next thought, let alone tomorrow's thoughts. Thoughts simply appear freely in the vast open space of life. They float in and out of awareness like clouds in the sky. Even in the midst of the noisiest thoughts, there is something here that is very quiet—something that is deeply at peace. It's what you are. It watches all thoughts as they come and go. It *allows* all thoughts to come and go.

You can't know your next thought. You don't even have the power to *not* think about something. When you try to *not* think about something, what happens? That thought, that image appears—it has to. You can't *not* think about something. The very fact that you know what you shouldn't be thinking about means that thought is already appearing, even if you don't want to admit that to yourself or to anyone else!

This is one of the many illusions that we hold: that we are the thinkers of our thoughts. The reality is, thoughts simply appear in the vast silence that you are, and it's only another thought that says, "I thought that thought!" Thoughts are impersonal, but we believe that they are owned by us. So now we appear to have two things: a thought and a me who thinks it, the thinker of the thought. But this is an assumption and nothing more. In reality, you never experience this split between thinker and thought; you simply find thoughts coming and going in what you are. There is no thinker that thinks a thought; there is simply a thought appearing now. "I am the thinker" is only another thought!

This is the essence of true meditation: to simply relax back into the vast open space in which thoughts come and go and to notice that thoughts are not personal.

Now imagine this: A little kid goes up to his parents and says, "Mummy, Daddy, I had a thought! My brother is going to die because he won't let me play on the computer!" The parents reply, "No! That's a very bad thought! You shouldn't think that! You're bad for thinking that! Evil child! No supper tonight! Go to your room!" What they are implying is that the child thought the thought—that he is responsible for having that thought. There is a *bad* thinker of thoughts, and that bad thinker is not okay and must be punished. Their assumption is this: if a "bad" thought appears (a thought they judge as bad), a bad thinker must have produced it.

From the child's perspective, he didn't choose to have the thought. It just appeared out of nowhere. It was an expression of anger toward his brother, anger that had not been deeply accepted in present experience. When anger is not deeply accepted here and now, we move into the story of "I am an angry *person*," forgetting who we really are. And then the angry *person*, seeking release from the discomfort of unaccepted anger, gets angry at another person. "I want to hit my brother" simply means "I am very angry with my brother—so angry that in this moment and only in this moment, I *feel* that I want to hit him. And I'm trying to communicate this to you. I am simply seeking *okayness*."

But now the child has been told that there is a *bad* thinker producing *bad* thoughts. It's almost like being told you're possessed by the devil (or at least that there is something fundamentally wrong with you). There's an evil thinker thinking evil thoughts. There's a sinner thinking sinful thoughts. Your brain is dysfunctional, and it is producing sick thoughts.

And so the child thinks to himself, "I mustn't have bad thoughts (even though on some level I know that I didn't choose to have the thoughts in the first place). I mustn't be bad, because Mummy and Daddy don't love me when I'm bad."

Now the bad thoughts—and possibly the anger—are going to be repressed in some way. "Thoughts about people dying, thoughts about hurting people, unkind thoughts about others are not okay. Mummy and Daddy told me so, and I don't want to risk losing their love and approval by having those thoughts."

And so the war with thought begins.

It doesn't always happen the way I've described in this dramatic example, but as we grow up, all of us are conditioned to believe that certain thoughts are bad, dark, unhealthy, sick, sinful, and negative and, more importantly, that we are the *thinkers* of those nasty thoughts. Some thoughts I simply shouldn't be having. Some thoughts are fundamentally not okay. And so we try our hardest to banish these thoughts, to make them go away.

Perhaps we go to war with our thoughts because of another superstition. Just as we believe that if we feel something for too long or too intensely or even at all, we will be it or become it, so we believe, "If I think it, it will come true. If I think it, it will happen. If I think it, I will attract it. If I think it, I will become it. If I think it, my parents will find out (or my teacher will find out or my boss will find out or my guru will find out or my partner will find out or God will find out), and I will be punished. If I think it, people will *know* that I am thinking it, and they will judge me. They will see me for who I really am, and I will be rejected by the world. I will be seen as the impure, imperfect being that I am."

If they find out what I'm thinking, they won't love me.

I once met a woman with a huge smile. She told me what a positive person she was. She was the most positive person in the world! She was so positive, and she spread positivity wherever she went. She lit up the universe with her positivity. She was a beacon of love and joy and happiness. In her own words, she was a "light being."

There was just one thing that troubled her—a strange negative "entity," a kind of unhappy ghost, who followed her around constantly. Wherever she was, whomever she was talking to, whatever she was doing, he was always there, right next to her, spreading his negative energy, filling her head with negative thoughts. She couldn't understand why he was there and why he wouldn't go away. She was such a positive person; why did she deserve to have a miserable apparition as a stalker? She had tried everything to make him disappear, but he wouldn't budge. Why couldn't she make the ghost disappear?

The entity was herself, as you might have guessed. All the parts of herself that she found too negative, all of those waves that didn't fit in with her "I'm the most positive person in the world" identity (image), were projected onto this unhappy ghost, whom she then experienced as being outside of herself: "The negativity is not in me—it's in him!"

Do you see the brilliance of the seeker here? What doesn't fit into our image of ourselves we banish in some way. The woman was not aware that this was what she was doing, and in working with her, I helped her see that there was no ghost outside of her—that, in fact, she was the ghost. And she came to see that the negativity was okay, that there was truth in it, and that it was not a threat to who she was. She simply needed to love the ghost to death—to integrate him into what she was. She would come to discover that who she really was allowed all positivity and all negativity. Who she really was was beyond both polarities. And in that place, there was no need to hold up a positive-person image, or any image, in fact.

In a way, we are all like this dear woman, banishing the waves of experience that don't fit with how we want to see ourselves and how we want to be seen. When we want to hold up a positive image of ourselves, it is inevitable that we go to war with what we perceive as negative.

However, who you really are does not distinguish between positive and negative thoughts; it does not *see* positive and negative. *All* thoughts are allowed to come and go in what you are. You can project any movie onto a movie screen—a romantic comedy; a war epic; a horror flick; a "positive," happy movie or an upsetting, "negative" movie—and the screen remains untouched. The screen cannot be damaged by any of the movies that appear on it. You are like this movie screen—it cannot be hurt, contaminated, corrupted, or broken by any thought, however "negative." Any and all thoughts are allowed on the screen of awareness. You are not the thinker; the thoughts simply appear.

When a thought such as "I'm a waste of space" or "I'm a total failure" or even a violent one such as "I hate my friend" or "I wish he was dead" appears, a kind of panic can set in: "I shouldn't be thinking that. My goodness, where did that thought come from? Maybe there's something wrong with me. I'm a good person! I love my friend. I would never wish that upon him. Oh God, maybe that thought means that I'm actually going to kill him! Oh no. I'm not a killer, am I? My goodness, I need to get rid of that thought. That thought isn't me. It's evil!" We believe the thought "I shouldn't have had that thought" and we suffer.

We are afraid that thinking about something will lead to it becoming real, but as I have said, this is superstition. The truth is, the more I simply *allow* a thought to appear, the less likely it is that I will end up acting it out. The more I try to ignore the thought, to repress it, to destroy it, the more I go to war against it, the more I battle against myself, and the more it feels like I might actually end up doing what I fear doing. The more I go to war internally, the more likely that war will express itself in the world.

We see this dynamic at work in the father who had angry outbursts at his children. In his helplessness, in his desperation and his inability to control his kids, the father had all sorts of thoughts—thoughts a father "should never have." He had thoughts about hurting his kids, even about killing them, even about killing himself (and it took real courage and brutal honesty for the father to admit to me that he'd had such thoughts). He had thoughts that you're supposed to keep to yourself; thoughts you think nobody else has; thoughts that make you think there's something wrong with you.

Those "violent" thoughts arose, and the father was shocked at himself for thinking such things. What a bad, evil, vicious thinker he was! The thoughts went against everything he believed—everything he stood for as a father, as a man, as a human being. And yet, they appeared, and they weren't in his control.

And that's when the panic would really set in. "Oh my God, I shouldn't be thinking that! What's wrong with me? I'm the worst father in the world. I'm a failed father. I'm a terrible person. I'm so far from spiritual awakening! I'm sick! How do I stop these thoughts? How can I get rid of them? How can I destroy them? Maybe I'm mentally ill! Help! *Help!*"

And at that point of total panic and helplessness, he lashed out at his children. Again, lashing out is a way to get relief and release from "dangerous" thoughts. The irony is, the real danger is in the lashing out to escape the thoughts—not in the thoughts themselves. The thoughts are innocent; it's in our judgment and rejection of thoughts that the trouble begins.

The thought "I want to kill my children" doesn't fit the image of a good father! These are not the kinds of thoughts a father—or anyone for that matter—is supposed to have. But the truth was, in that moment, those thoughts *were* appearing. That was the *reality*. And who wants to deny reality, however troubling it is? Only the seeker. The seeker thrives on denial. To come out of denial and simply *admit* what is true can be terrifying to the seeker, for it destroys the image the seeker is trying to uphold.

Deep down, the man knew that he would never lay a finger on his children, but still the "bad" thoughts appeared—an expression of his frustration and helplessness, his desperation to control the situation. The seeker was looking for a way out of the discomfort, and the mind went to an extreme: "If I killed my kids, I would be at peace." The seeker was becoming desperate for an escape, and desperate thoughts were appearing. The thought was quickly labeled an "evil" thought, a "sick" thought, an "unhealthy" thought. And because there was the assumption that he had thought it, now not only was this father unable to control his children, but he was also an evil father, a sick man, a terrible person, not fit to have children, not fit to live. Suffering on top of suffering.

If he had simply allowed that thought to be there, it's unlikely that the panic would have set in, that he would have become so angry with himself, that he would have been so frightened, and that he would have ended up screaming at his children in helplessness. We are afraid to allow the most "negative" thoughts, because we are afraid of what they *say about us,* and we somehow imagine that allowing them to be there, in the space of who we are, will mean they will take us over. In fact, it's the other way around—when we reject thoughts, try to escape them, and punish ourselves for thinking them, they tend to grow and grow and grow in size and in importance. The seeking, the desperation to escape, becomes so intense that even the most seemingly peaceful person can end up becoming violent. Think of those television news reports about an ordinary person who has gone on a killing spree. When the reporters interview friends and acquaintances of the killer, they say, "But he seemed such a calm, gentle man ..."

It's very strange, but in the total allowing of violent thoughts, violence ends. *True peace is not at war with violence.* The movie screen has no preference. A positive movie, a negative movie, a loving movie, a violent movie—they are all allowed to come and go on the screen. *A violent movie doesn't make the screen more violent.* The screen never panics, because it knows that all thoughts are allowed to play out on it.

All of these thoughts that we reject simply wouldn't be a problem if we weren't trying to hold up an image of ourselves. "I'm a nonviolent person." "I'm a positive person." "I'm a happy person." "I'm a 100-percent-loving light being." Wonderful! But that image means that you will go to war with any thought that doesn't fit that image.

If you're trying to hold up an image of yourself as a positive person, you most likely won't allow negative thoughts. A successful person might not allow herself to have thoughts about failure. An enlightened, spiritual person perhaps won't allow himself to have unenlightened, nonspiritual thoughts—angry thoughts, sexual thoughts, fearful thoughts. People who are trying to be pure won't allow any thought they have been conditioned to believe is impure. Or even worse, if they see themselves as enlightened beings who have transcended thoughts entirely, then they won't allow themselves to have thoughts at all. The moment you hold up *any* image of yourself, you will be in conflict with thoughts. The most nonviolent individuals will go to war with thoughts that threaten their nonviolent image of themselves. We go to war in defense of images, and images always seem to be threatened by thoughts.

We talk a lot about "positive" and "negative" thoughts, but now we see that there is no such thing as negative thoughts. The thought "I am ugly" is not a negative thought. It is a thought that we label as negative because we don't like what it says about us. The thought "I am ugly" upsets us because we don't want to admit ugliness into our experience. The thought "I am a failure" upsets us because we don't want to deeply embrace failure, since that embrace would threaten our image of ourselves as a successful person. We try to banish all "negative" thoughts and have only "positive" thoughts.

Positive thinking has become quite a craze in recent years. But this tactic ultimately doesn't work, because the opposites *always* arise together. Most often, when we think we are thinking positively, we are really just *covering up* negative with positive. The negative is still there, rumbling underneath, ready to spoil all our fun when we least expect it! We feel ugly, that ugly feeling is not accepted, and so we try to suffocate the ugliness by trying to think and feel "positively." But our beauty is then hollow and superficial, both to ourselves and others, and doesn't provide what we truly long for.

You could say that in seeking the positive, we actually create the negative. They cannot exist without each other. Positive thinking actually creates negative thinking.

Some people report that they feel attacked or plagued by negative thoughts. Remember, though, that what we are cannot be attacked—only an image can. So any time you experience a thought as being negative, any time you feel personally attacked, it is a sign that you are defending an image of yourself. When no image of yourself is being defended, all thoughts are allowed to arise and fall away. Then you see that all thoughts are true—in other words, all thoughts have truth in them. If you are honest you can find *everything* in yourself—and then thought cannot be your enemy. Every thought you call "negative" is actually a dear friend, trying to show you the false image of yourself that you are still defending.

It's almost as if life, in its infinite compassion, attempts to destroy any false image you have of yourself. If you hold onto beautiful, ugly will come along and attempt to destroy it. If you hold onto successful, failure will start to batter you until you see reality. It's almost as if life wants to be in perfect balance—it wants beautiful *and* ugly, not just one or the other. It wants everything, because it is everything. So perhaps what we experience as a negative thought is simply life trying to balance itself out. If we really listen to suffering, it *always* shows us what we're still at war with. It *always* shows us what we are seeking.

So the thought "I am ugly" is simply an invitation to deeply allow feelings of ugliness. The thought "I am a failure" invites us to deeply allow feelings of failure in the moment. So easily we forget who we are, as the vast capacity for life itself, and go to war with a thought, labeling it as "negative," rather than seeing its inherent truth. If we are open, we can always find the truth in a thought, even the most "negative" thoughts about ourselves. We come to see that we are not who we think we are. We are unlimited and free, vast enough to contain all of life.

Often you are trying to protect an image of yourself and don't even realize it. A woman once told me how "free from identity" she was. She had studied nonduality—Advaita—for years, learned from dozens of famous teachers, had all sorts of awakening experiences, and finally had come to shed her entire identity. She was no longer someone. She was now no one. She was free from all images. She was simply an open space of awareness. She had gone beyond all roles—mother, wife, daughter, spiritual seeker.

There was one thing that was bothering her, though.

"It's my children!" she said. "I just don't understand them. They see me as their mother! Can't they see I'm not really their mother? Can't they see that ultimately I'm nothing and nobody?" She told me how her children's inability to accept her view of reality was causing much suffering and confusion in her life, which further confused her, because she thought that after "awakening," you weren't supposed to get confused! "If they could just see who I really am!" she said. "Can't they see I'm not really their mother? Can't they see I'm free from all identity? Can't they see I have no story about myself anymore?"

I said, "But you *do* have a story. Your story is that you have no story. You are completely identified with *not* being their mother. And every time your children call you Mother, it's a threat to your identity, your image of 'I am not a mother.' That's why it hurts when they call you Mother. Their image conflicts with yours."

She realized where all her suffering was coming from: she was seeking something her children couldn't give her. She was mentally at war with them, in her attempt to hold up her image of herself as "non-mother." She had stopped listening to her children. She thought she was free from identity, free from seeking, and yet seeking was still going on.

Yes, even a spiritual identity such as "I have no identity" or "I am nobody" can become yet another identity, another trap, another image to hold up, another story to defend. If you hold up an image of yourself as nobody, you'll secretly go to war with anyone who doesn't buy into that image. You'll start saying things like "I am nobody, but you're still somebody," and there will be inner conflict. The defense of an image always leads to conflict and, therefore, suffering—no matter how "awakened" you think you are. It was this woman's suffering that pointed her back home in the end. All images crumble in the face of life.

Which thoughts and judgments, from yourself and from others, hurt? Which thoughts do you perceive as negative? Can this perception tell you which images of yourself you are still defending in the moment? Where do you go to war in defense of a false image of yourself? Which waves of experience are you trying to protect yourself from? What are you not allowing in? And is it possible to recognize that what you are not allowing in has already been allowed in?

All suffering, all conflict, contains within it an invitation to cease to identify yourself as an image and to discover the deepest acceptance in present experience.

We have now covered the basics of seeking:

- Experiencing ourselves as separate waves in the ocean and not seeing completeness in our present experience, we *seek completeness* in the future.

- Money, sex, enlightenment, fame, beauty—which of these symbolizes the end of seeking to you? We give these things *power;* they seem to have the power to bring completeness. And so we mystify them, long for them, follow them, worship them, want to become them. We become addicted to a future wholeness. But we fail to find what we are really looking for until we discover who we really are, in this present moment.

- We try to escape certain experiences—ugliness, weakness, failure, helplessness—any experience we deem to be a threat to completeness. But these are not actually threats to completeness. As waves in the ocean, they are *already deeply accepted,* and all we need to do is recognize this acceptance in the moment. All thoughts and feelings are allowed to come and go in what you are.

- Deep acceptance is not something you *achieve*—it's what you *are* in your essence. What you are is the *open space* in which all waves of experience are allowed to come and go. The open space is inseparable from all that appears within it. It is the ocean, inseparable from all its waves. This is the intimacy and love we have always longed for— an intimacy right at the heart of our present experience.

- As open space, you cannot be defined by any of the apparent opposites—good, evil, healthy, unhealthy, enlightened, unenlightened. We run away from the negative and try to reach the positive, and this attempt to escape life we call *suffering*. Suffering is always an invitation to discover, in the moment, what we are not deeply accepting and to see that what we are not accepting is already accepted.

• As open space, what you are is not the seeker; you are that which sees the seeking play itself out. You are not an incomplete entity that is trying to complete itself in time. The end of seeking is not something that the seeker will find in the future. You *are* the end of seeking, now. You *are* what you seek, in this moment.

The metaphor of the seeking mechanism has astonishing explanatory power. It can help us to understand suffering that otherwise may seem incomprehensible to us. Understanding the basics of this mechanism, we will now look in more detail at how this dynamic manifests in our everyday lives.

For the rest of the book, building on some of the ideas and insights we have talked about, we will be exploring the seeking that's happening in our most intimate relationships—how we seek love and acceptance from other people, and how it leads to conflict, inauthenticity, dishonesty, and strained communication. We will see how the seeking mechanism gives rise to addictions and unhealthy repetitive behaviors, and how in our seeking we end up giving away our own power and submit to the rule of others—to gurus, to cult leaders, to people we perceive as powerful but who have no real power. We will see how suffering is created as we try to escape physical pain, and how the rejection of the present moment leads to everything that we call violent and evil in the world.

We will also see how we can find the deepest acceptance even in the places we thought it could never be. We will find the light even in the darkest of places—the light that we are, enlightenment itself.

In exposing the seeker in all its subtle and not-so-subtle manifestations, in shining the light on the seeker in all aspects of this human experience, we will come to see how we have been creating unnecessary suffering for ourselves and others, and at the same time, we will find a way out of that suffering. The way out of suffering is the way in. See if you can recognize yourself in any of the situations presented in the following pages. If you are a human being like me, I'm sure you will be able to relate to what I am going to tell you!

You cannot find yourself in the past or future. The only place where you can find yourself is in the Now. To be a seeker implies that you need the future. If this is what you believe, it becomes true for you: you will need time until you realize that you don't need time to be who you are.

ECKHART TOLLE

Part II

DEEP ACCEPTANCE IN EVERYDAY LIFE

Pain and Illness

I was once having a conversation with a doctor who worked primarily with people who had been diagnosed with cancer. He spent a large amount of his time with people who often were in extreme physical pain. He was asking me how he could begin to integrate his interest in the physical healing of his patients with his desire to help them recognize who they really are, beyond their story of themselves as cancer patients who needed healing. He said that often he felt torn between helping them with their physical pain and wanting to help them go beyond their pain. He said to me, "You know, Jeff, I'm familiar with all the spiritual concepts—that there's no such thing as pain, pain is an illusion, we are not our bodies, there's nobody there, and so on—but how does that actually *help* people who are struggling with extreme pain?"

The doctor was making a very important point. All of those spiritual concepts ("There is no me," "I am not the body," "Pain is an illusion," "There is no death") are very beautiful and can, when heard and used in the right way, really help to point back to the ever-present freedom in the midst of every experience, *including* the most painful ones.

However, at the same time, these concepts can easily be *misunderstood—and misused*. They can be used to actually *deny* our present experience and, therefore, cause us to suffer more than ever. The concept "There is no pain" can simply be a way for seekers to *avoid* feeling the pain they feel in the moment! The concept "This is not my body" can be used to *avoid* facing uncomfortable thoughts and feelings they have about their body. The concept "There is no self" or "Everything is impersonal" can be used to *deny* intimate, and very personal, human feelings and emotions, which are simply asking to be deeply embraced in the impersonal space that you are. The phenomenon of using spiritual concepts to deny unacceptable human emotions and feelings has often been called "spiritual bypassing."

Similarly, telling someone who is in terrible pain that "there is no pain; there is only Oneness" can be a way to invalidate *their* present-moment experience—even if your intention is good. It can be a way to make them "wrong" and you "right." Telling them these things can actually be a form of arrogance on your part. The shadow side of spiritual teachings is that the mind can easily use them to deny reality—and then deny that it is denying reality! Real spirituality has nothing to do with this kind of denial. Real spirituality is the end of denial. And we come out of denial totally when we simply admit the truth of this moment, however painful that admission may feel, however much it destroys our dreams.

I told the doctor that if I were talking to someone in intense physical pain, possibly the last thing they would want—or be able—to hear is "It's not your pain." The truth is that their pain, in this moment, is real to them, and if we are to begin to find the wholeness within present experience, we must first *validate* and *honor* that present experience, no matter how illusory we perceive it to be, and, from there, move to find out what is really true. I meet you in your dream, and we explore the dream together, coming to see through it.

If someone is suffering, simply telling them that they are not really suffering or that suffering is an illusion doesn't end the suffering. If you are suffering, simply believing that you are an awakened nobody and, therefore, are not suffering doesn't change a thing. Remember that a wave might *ultimately* be the ocean, but it *still appears to be a wave.* And by ignoring or invalidating the appearance of the wave, you are actually rejecting the ocean itself.

Freedom is always about what's true, right now—not what I think is true, not what I've been told is true, not what I believe is true, not what my spiritual teacher told me was true, but what is *actually* true in this moment, in this present experience, in *these* thoughts, *these* sensations, *these* feelings. True freedom is about admitting what's true. And what's true right now is that the pain damn well *hurts*—whether the pain is mine or not, whether it is real or all just a dream, whether there is somebody here or nobody here, whether there is oneness or twoness or threeness or anything else— and all the clever mental trickery in the world isn't going to stop the pain in *this* moment. You cannot intellectualize, philosophize, or think your way out of pain. Simply adding the belief "You are not the body" or "There's nobody here" on top of the painful experience isn't going to make the situation any more okay. Such beliefs are just other roles to take on, other religions. You're not okay, but you have to pretend that you're okay in order to seem spiritual or enlightened. You're suffering, but you have to pretend that you are not, so you can continue to hold up an image of yourself as someone who has transcended suffering. How exhausting!

No, the freedom I talk about has nothing to do with escaping life as it is or pretending to be something that you're not. It has everything to do with total, radical honesty—seeing reality as it is, *admitting* it in both senses of the word. *Admit* is a beautiful word—it means both "tell the truth" and "allow in." To *admit* present experience—to tell the truth about what is actually present—is to recognize that what's present has already been *admitted* into life. The waves appearing at present have already been *admitted* into the ocean, and *admitting* that they exist is at the absolute core of this teaching. Waking up is all about admitting who you really are!

True healing is not about escaping suffering and reaching wholeness at some point in the future—it's about seeing that wholeness here, right now, at the very heart of suffering. It is not surprising that the words *whole* and *heal* share the same root. To heal is to rediscover wholeness here and now. Yes, true healing has nothing to do with escaping pain and reaching a future wholeness; true healing is actually here *in* the pain, however paradoxical and counterintuitive that may sound at first.

You will not become healed "one day" (that's the voice of the seeker again); you are already healed. What you are is already whole, even if you don't realize it, just as the wave in the ocean is already inseparable from that very ocean. Even in your pain, you are healed.

Like the spiritual beliefs discussed earlier, these are very beautiful words. But how do we *recognize* that healing even in the midst of the most painful experiences? Because simply *believing* that we are already healed isn't enough.

THE DIFFERENCE BETWEEN PAIN AND SUFFERING

Before we go any further in our discussion about healing, I think it's very important to distinguish between pain and suffering. What, exactly, are we trying to heal: the pain or the suffering?

I once spoke to a woman who was in a lot of pain and who had been given a few weeks to live. She had been a spiritual seeker her whole life. She had studied with many different spiritual teachers and had even lived for several years in an ashram in India in her pursuit of enlightenment. She considered herself to be fairly evolved spiritually, but now, in the face of her illness, that whole façade was crumbling. She told me that she felt like a total failure. After all of those years of spiritual seeking, all of that work on herself, all of those insights, she was *still* unable to be deeply okay with what was happening to her. In the midst of her pain, her image of herself was falling apart.

She experienced terrible fear over whether or not she'd be alive the next day, frustration about the state of her body (she felt let down by it), regret about all the things she'd never accomplished in her life, and a deep sadness about all the things she'd miss out on when she died. What had happened to all her ideas about equanimity in the face of life challenges? What happened to her conviction that she was totally present and positive in each and every moment? What happened to the idea that an awakened person experiences total peace even in the midst of devastation? What happened to her conviction that she was "nobody"? She felt like a failure and a fraud in the face of the reality of life as it was presenting itself to her. She felt humiliated by life. She'd thought she'd had life worked out, but now everything she knew had been cast into doubt.

Her enlightened façade was crumbling. How wonderful! All mind-made façades crumble in the end. This was life's invitation to go beyond her image of herself and discover who she really was in this moment. Not tomorrow, not yesterday, but this moment.

When things had been going well for her—when she was fit and healthy and full of energy—it was easy for her to feel enlightened and to say things like "This is not my body" and "There is no self." But now, lying in bed all day, weak and aching and dependent on medication to keep her alive, she felt like all her spiritual progress had been flushed down the toilet. She told me that she felt like she had regressed back to the way she'd been before she started spiritual seeking. She felt like a baby again, totally unable to cope with life, totally identified with her physical body, and she felt incredibly angry at herself for "failing like this." Why wasn't she able to be more "present," more "awake" to the situation, more okay? She felt she was clearly unawakened and had been kidding herself for the past thirty years. And so she lay in bed, day after day, mentally beating herself up for not being more spiritually evolved than she was.

This sweet woman was very attached to her concepts and beliefs about awakening and enlightenment. She had a very fixed idea about what awakening should look like. She had picked up the concept that an awakened person should feel good all the time or happy all the time or peaceful all the time or even okay all the time, and these secondhand beliefs were causing incredible amounts of suffering for her, making her feel like a total failure and a fraud. Remember, feeling something "all the time" is simply not possible in the ocean that you are.

The pain and physical weakness she could just about deal with, but it was the failure (death) of her identity that was upsetting her more than anything. It was all the shoulds and the shouldn'ts that she had picked up over the years, all the ideas about what this moment should look like that hurt, perhaps more than the pain itself. She was trying desperately to be okay with things as they were, but the reality was, she felt not okay and was beating herself up terribly because of it. She was desperately trying to hold herself together, and yet the pain was threatening to tear her reality apart. And every day was a battle to hold onto her identity.

It was the *stories* she was telling about her pain—how bad it was, how much worse it would get, how it would end up killing her—that made her situation feel intolerable, unbearable, desperate. It was her identity as a woman in pain that was the real burden—not the pain itself. Her story about herself as a *victim* of pain, as someone *imprisoned* by pain, as someone *trapped* in pain and unable to find a way out—*that* was her suffering; *that's* what needed healing. Her suffering was in her frustrated attempts to mentally escape the moment, her desperate need to be in control, and her failure to do so. Her suffering was her lack of deep acceptance of her total vulnerability in the face of life.

Physical pain has a way of pointing us, in the most dramatic way possible, to reality. Physical pain can really help us break through all images, if we are willing to really *feel* into it.

We say, "I'm in pain right now." But what do we really mean by that? Let's try to break apart our *story* of pain and get back to what's really happening in the moment. (And ultimately, everything I'm saying applies not only to physical pain but all kinds of emotional pain too—fear, anger, sadness, guilt, jealousy, frustration, boredom, grief. Pain is what *hurts* in the moment.)

Come back to present experience, to what is actually happening right now. What is here? All sorts of thoughts, feelings, sounds, and sensations are appearing and disappearing in what you are.

Go to the pain. And for a moment, as an experiment, drop the story of pain—drop your conclusions, your assumptions, everything you know about pain, your descriptions of it, your memories of your past experiences of it. And instead, explore this *present* experience, as if for the first time. What is actually here, beyond your ideas about what is here? What is the truth of this moment?

You may start to notice that what you have been calling pain isn't really pain at all. What do I mean by that? I mean there is nothing there that is static, solid, separate, fixed; you can't find anything solid called pain. Even if the pain feels very solid, look closer—and then closer still. As we have seen, in reality, present-moment experience is never fixed. A wave is really always moving, even if it looks stationary from a distance. We say, "That's a wave, and I know what a wave is," but by the time you've said that, the wave isn't the same wave. Words seem to fix things, but reality is never fixed. It's always a new wave and another new wave. Reality is always changing shape. The moment you try to describe a wave, saying, "It's like this" or "It's like that," the moment has already gone, the shape of the wave has already changed, and what you said a moment ago is no longer applicable to *this* moment.

Life moves, and thought always struggles to catch up. Life always comes before thought. In a sense, every thought is an *afterthought!*

So come back to these waves of experience, come back to what you call pain, and notice how it's not solid, but actually consists of all sorts of *smaller* waves, all kinds of changing sensations, moving, dancing. The moment you come to a mental conclusion about a sensation, in a sense you've stopped seeing and feeling, really *feeling*, what's actually there. You've moved into a mental story about your experience. So come back to what's actually happening and take another look now.

Drop your conclusion that what you are experiencing is called pain, and rediscover what is actually here. What are the sensations that you call pain actually like? Feel them—really feel into them. Give them direct, loving attention, without expecting them to change in any way and without trying to make them go away. Meet what's here without hope. Are the sensations static, solid, fixed, or do they move and dance in present experience? How do they move? Do they move quickly or slowly? Where are they going? Follow them. Do they feel like they are going in a specific direction or all kinds of directions at once? Are they traveling in little circles, going up and down, side to side, or in and out? Do the sensations have sharp edges, like little razors? Or do they feel softer, more rounded, more tender? Do they feel deep or shallow? Do the sensations have textures or patterns? Are they rough, smooth, bumpy, lumpy, prickly? Do they vibrate, throb, flutter, tremble, undulate, oscillate, shiver, pulsate, or palpitate? Do they have a rhythm, a beat? Do they have a temperature? Do they feel burning hot? Warm? Cold or icy? Are the sensations confined to a certain area, constricted in some way, locked in? Or do they flow freely, like water? Do they feel gloopy, liquidy, hard, thick, dull, syrupy, tickly, spiky? Are there any colors, shapes, or sounds associated with the sensations? Are the sensations red, purple, orange, yellow, green? Are they black, white, or transparent? Are they circular, square, triangular, oblong, or something else entirely? Do the sensations sing, squeal, or hum, or are they silent? Are they shy or confident? Do they feel young or old?

Don't be certain about what is here; don't pretend that you know. Always be an *explorer*. Always become intimate with what is actually present. Give loving attention to these poor little waves that have been rejected, neglected, homeless, and unloved for so long, and in doing so, notice that they are all allowed to be here. What you are has already allowed them in, no matter how strange or uncomfortable they appear to be. Sensations are not your enemies, however intense they feel.

When you go beyond the word *pain*—a word that carries so much baggage—what do you actually find for yourself, in your own present experience? You never find a generic, static, unmoving lump called pain. Pain is never a thing in your body. It's always much more *alive* than that. The actual experience is always infinitely richer than the story about that experience. You never find a thing; you find a dance of present-moment sensations, shapes, textures, temperatures, which, in the end, you cannot put into words. Even the words I have used above—*sharp, soft, warm*—are still just descriptions. Perhaps they seem to get a little closer to the actual experience, but they are still just descriptions, and even they don't capture what's really going on. Simply relax *all* descriptions, and explore from there.

Without the story, do you really have any way of knowing what pain is?

And we can go even further: *without the story, do you really have any way of knowing what sensations actually are?*

Without the story, life is a total mystery, isn't it? Yes, the mystery is there even within the experience of pain. Pain does not destroy or block mystery; it is saturated with mystery. Even pain is *made* of mystery. Even pain is *made* of consciousness. Everything is made of what you are.

And notice, in this place beyond the story, you cannot say that these sensations are happening inside something called "my body." Another one of our many assumptions about reality is that sensations happen inside a body. But when you come back to your own present experience of life, can you actually find this solid and separate body in which the sensations are supposed to be happening? Or do you simply find an incredibly alive dance of present-moment sensations, a tingling, amorphous mass with impossible-to-detect boundaries, appearing in the unlimited and unboundaried capacity that you are? Is "the body" simply another idea, an image, a picture, a thought, a memory, also appearing in what you are? Can the thought or image of "my body" ever begin to touch the incredible aliveness and immediacy of present experience? Can the vastness of present experience ever be reduced to a thought?

If you ask somebody to stop for a moment, close their eyes, and *feel* their body—really feel into their arms, legs, feet, chest, teeth, and tongue—and describe to you what they feel, they will almost inevitably begin to tell you a story about their body. Instead of feeling their arms, legs, feet, chest, teeth, and tongue right now, instead of really being there with those sensations, exploring them, becoming intimate with them, dropping all descriptions and finding their own inseparability from them and intimacy with them, they will start *thinking* about their arms, legs, feet, chest, teeth, and tongue. They will be lost in *images* and *pictures* of their body, in memories, in what they *know* rather than giving their body direct attention, rather than really coming back to present sensations. They will think *about* their body; they will talk *about and around* it, rather than feel everything directly in this moment.

What does your right hand feel like, right now?

Did you suddenly get an image of your right hand and start describing that image? Did you feel your hand for a moment and then fall into generic descriptions of feelings? It's easier to describe an image rather than put into words the mystery of what a foot feels like, or what an arm feels like, or what a head-ache feels like. Who can really capture the mystery of a headache in words? Maybe that's why we go so quickly to our stories—they are somehow easier, safer. Perhaps we want to give someone else the "right" answer. Perhaps reverting to our stories is part of our search for a consistent self. Who knows?

Often, when you ask people to tell you about their pain or discomfort, they will launch straight into a story *about* their pain, rather than actually feeling the pain right now. They will talk *around* their pain, rather than *from* it. They will tell you how bad the pain is, how much it hurts, how much better or worse it is than yesterday's pain, how upset they are about it, how much it is getting in the way of their plans, how terrible or wonderful their care has been, and so on. Telling a story about past pain, about future pain, about everything they know about pain, comparing their pain to other peoples' pain, are wonderful ways to avoid *feeling pain* right now.

The story is always a pale imitation of what is actually happening, a "pale imitation of the celebration," as I call it. Every story is massively reductive; it attempts to reduce the mystery of life to a few words. For example, right now, you may be sitting on a chair or lying in bed. "I'm sitting on a chair" or "I'm lying in bed" is the story about your experience. Drop that story. What is it actually like, in this moment, here where you are? The story is that the body is lying or sitting, but if we drop that story for a moment and come back to the actual present-moment sensations, what is here? What is happening right now, in the immediacy of present experience? Come back to the tingles, the warmth, and the throb of present sensation. Can this present experience really ever be captured by words or images?

When we come back to our actual present-moment experience and drop all conclusions, all stories, and start again, as it were, exploring our experience with the innocence of a newborn baby, we simply find this amazing dance of sensations, never the same from one moment to the next. Reality is always far more mysterious, far more unknowable, than our story about reality. And we say, "These sensations are happening inside my body" without investigating whether or not that is true. In the story, pain is happening to *me*. In the story, pain is located inside my body. In reality, there is an astonishing, ever-changing dance of sensation going on in what I am.

In reality, sensations simply dance in the space that you are—the space of awareness itself. You don't experience sensations as being inside as opposed to outside, do you? They are simply here, present, alive. Isn't it an extra thought added on afterwards that these sensations are "in my body"? Can you actually find that boundary, that gap, that division, between inside and outside the body, here in this present experience? Close your eyes. Come back to the amorphous mass of dancing sensations right now. Isn't the idea that you have a body at all simply another image appearing in this space? Drop that image for a moment, and come back to the actual experience. There's just present-moment sensation, isn't there? When we drop the idea that sensations happen inside a body, we are now aligned with reality.

Now, since thought operates in the world of opposites, the moment it labels present sensation as "pain," it immediately starts to compare and contrast it with something called "pleasure" or "lack of pain." And so there is already a judgment built into the word *pain*. Pain is now the opposite of something, and for many people, the word *pain* has all sorts of negative connotations: Pain is bad. Pain means danger. Pain is evil. Pain is a punishment from God. Pain means I am unloved. Pain means I am weak. Pain means I have failed. Pain means there is something wrong with me. *Pain* is a very *heavy* word. You could say that by the time we even call it pain, we've stopped seeing what's really there. We've moved into a story about what's there. You could say that calling it pain is the first layer of illusion. Hidden in that word are all sorts of judgments, beliefs, and fears. The label *pain* is really a judgment, an opinion, not a thing that exists separately from you.

The second layer of illusion is the ownership of pain. "Pain" becomes "my pain." (This illusion of ownership can also apply to other feelings—"my fear," "my sadness," "my anger," "my boredom," "my confusion," and so on.) In the beginning, as we have seen, pain—or at least what we call pain—is just a bunch of sensations dancing in what we are. These sensations don't belong to anyone yet. They are deeply accepted by life, and they are not personal. Does anyone own a sensation? Does anyone own a sound? Does anyone own a feeling? Does anyone own a breath? Does anyone own the sound of a bird singing? Does anyone own the warmth of the sun on their face? Does anyone own life? When you see life for what it is, you see that none of it can be owned, because nobody can separate themselves from life. Nobody can turn around and say, "That is mine." Ownership is the second layer of illusion. Life itself, including even the most intimate and seemingly personal sensations, does not belong to anyone.

But we never stop to question this process, and so before you know it, quite literally, it's "my pain." When pain is not deeply accepted, we move into the story of "me and my pain": "The pain is mine." "I own pain." "I have pain." "I am *in* pain." "I am the one in pain." Whatever version we choose, that story now becomes our new identity. We become pain's victims. This is the beginning of our suffering around pain.

The whole seeking mechanism hinges on the illusion of separation and ownership—the idea that life happens to you. At the core of our suffering is the sense that something bad is happening *to* us. In fact, that's what the word *suffering* literally means—"to undergo or endure." There's a sense of passivity (from the Latin *passio,* meaning "I suffer"), of not being in control, of being the victim of life. But this passivity—the idea that life happens *to* you, that pain happens *to* you—is the illusion, the deceptive appearance. In reality, pain doesn't happen *to* you; it doesn't happen *to* a separate entity. It simply *appears* in what you are. Pain doesn't attack you; it dances in open space. The idea that it is happening *to* you is simply another idea appearing in what you are. In this sense, you could say that *pain is real, but suffering is the illusion, because suffering is the story that pain is happening to you, when in reality it isn't. Suffering, defined as the ownership of pain, is an illusion.*

The third layer of illusion is our attempt to escape pain. When the pain is not deeply accepted in this moment, I become "the one who is in pain." And then the search is on. I do not want to be the one who is in pain. I want to escape pain. I want to be "the one who is not in pain." I don't want to be pain's victim. I want a new identity! And so the one in pain starts looking for an escape from victimhood.

The mind, because it is dualistic, takes pain and creates the opposite concept: no pain. And now there is the attempt to move from pain (what is) to no pain (what is not). As we have seen, in reality there are no opposites.

This actual present-moment experience, as the dance of sensations, moment by moment, has no opposite. What we are really trying to do, in our seeking, is to move from present sensations to the absence of them. We try to move from present-moment pain to the image of no pain. Quite clearly, this is an impossible movement, because to escape pain and move to a place of no pain is going to require *time*. It is in this moment *right now* that I want to be free from pain. But life cannot give me what I want right now. I try to move from *here* to *not here* in this timeless moment. I try to move from *what is* to *what is not,* from *what is* to my image of *what should be*—and that is my suffering, that is my frustration, that is my despair.

Suffering is an attempt at an *impossible* movement, and that's why it hurts so much.

We believe that healing is the *absence* of pain, illness, discomfort. But true healing has nothing to do with escaping these waves of experience. The healing you really long for is the deepest acceptance of pain, the end of all illusions. The healing you really long for is the healing from your identity as the victim of pain. We don't really want to be free from pain; we want to be free from the image of ourselves as "the one who is in pain." We don't really want freedom *from* pain; we want the deepest acceptance *in* the pain.

Discovering yourself to be the wide-open space in which pain appears and not the story of someone who is being attacked by pain, that is true healing—the healing of identity—and it goes far beyond physical healing.

People in lots of pain often say things like, "It feels like my body has turned against me." But when you discover who you really are, you see it is not possible for your body to turn against you. A few years ago, I had an operation on a very sensitive part of my body and, as a result, lay in bed for several weeks in extreme pain. There was a sharp, stabbing feeling, and it often brought tears to my eyes. These days, as an intelligent human being, I know that *there is no point in experiencing more pain than I need to.* That's another one of those spiritual concepts that we pick up—the idea that the more we suffer, the closer we get to freedom. *Suffering is not the path to future freedom; suffering is an invitation to present freedom.* And so, naturally, I asked for medicine to reduce the pain. I was given morphine, and it certainly helped. Yet still the pain was there.

Often people ask me, "Jeff, if you really allowed everything, including pain, why would you ever take painkillers?" My reply is, "Everything is allowed here, *including* painkillers." Painkillers are part of life too. It doesn't seem intelligent to me to experience more pain than necessary. And if you do choose to not take painkillers, that's also okay.

In the end, neither painkillers nor the absence of painkillers leads to true healing, which is what we really long for and what this book is really about. Painkillers may be able to ease physical pain, but the real pain of life is in the suffering, the seeking, the identity, the attempt to control present experience. And there is no magic pill for that. There is no magic pill to end seeking. If there were, spiritual teachers, gurus, and therapists would have been out of their jobs many years ago.

No, this book is about the kind of healing that no substance or person (or lack of them) can give you—the wholeness that you are. Pills can numb sensation and feeling. Pills can alter brain chemistry. Pills can give you a high. But pills cannot and will never provide wholeness. Pills cannot bring deep acceptance. Perhaps they can make you more comfortable, but they cannot wake you up from your imagination of yourself.

Can the deepest acceptance of life be found within the experience of even the most extreme pain? Lying in bed, all of those years ago, with intense pain shooting through a very delicate region of my anatomy, what I discovered was that, on the deepest level, *the pain was okay*. It was a stunning realization that cut right to the heart of suffering. Pain was not the enemy. Pain was simply life appearing as pain—and beyond even this story, it was simply an ever-changing dance of sensations. The pain was not a block to life—it *was* life, in the moment. Pain was not in the way of life—it was a full and complete expression of life. Pain was deeply alive. It was the ocean appearing as a pain wave. The pain was still painful— let's not deny reality or pretend in any way. It still hurt, but on the deepest level, it was okay. It hurt, but I was not "the hurt one." It hurt, but in some incomprehensible way it could not hurt me. And it was allowed to be there for as long as it was there. It had a home in me.

It was quite shocking to realize the vastness, the total inclusivity, the all-encompassing nature of this deep acceptance. The pain was deeply okay—and what was also deeply okay was me, the character Jeff, not wanting it to be there. I think this is a huge misconception for spiritual seekers—that they, *personally,* need to be okay with everything that happens. What a huge burden it is to believe that you need to be okay with everything, all the time—to have to pretend that you are okay with everything even when you are not! As I've been saying, the deepest acceptance doesn't necessarily need you to be okay with the pain. Your not-okayness with the pain is totally embraced by life. This deep acceptance takes "you" out of the picture! It is a cosmic okayness that goes beyond "I'm okay" and "I'm not okay."

So the pain is there, and also what can appear is a dislike of, an aversion to, the pain. It was such a relief—and a revelation—to be able to lie in bed and to not have to hold up any image of myself, even an image of myself as an enlightened or awakened person, or as someone who was okay with pain! I was totally free to respond to the pain in an authentic, honest, human way again, after years of spiritual bypassing and pretending and denial. *I was free to say, "I don't like this pain," to admit a dislike of pain, and on a deeper level, to experience a total, all-embracing okayness with the entire situation.* Underneath everything, there is a cosmic okayness that cannot die.

It was not about simply *telling myself* that I was okay when I really wasn't. It wasn't about *pretending* to be okay. It wasn't about *trying* to be okay—trying to be spiritual, trying to be peaceful, trying to be anything other than what I was. It was about radical honesty. It was about seeing the pain, acknowledging it, admitting it, and discovering that the pain was fully admitted into life. In *admitting* the pain, the pain was *admitted*. And so there was pain, *and* Jeff didn't particularly like it. After all, who likes pain? Who would choose pain, if they had the choice?

Pain is such a wonderful teacher because it shows you that in the end, in the moment, *you have no choice.* You are not in control. "Not my will, but thy will be done," as Jesus said. And there is the liberation, right there.

The pain was embraced, as was the one trying and failing to escape the pain. The pain was embraced, as was the seeker of freedom from pain. And then where was the problem? *In* the pain, *in* the discomfort, I was whole. In the pain, in the extreme discomfort, I was healed—totally healed. Healed beyond comprehension. Healed beyond all understanding. Healed from the burden of being "the one in pain." Healed from the story of "my past and future pain." Healed from the illusion that the pain was happening to *me.* That healing didn't mean the pain went away immediately, but somehow that pain became secondary. This ever-present healing was what I had really been looking for.

"By his wounds we are healed," it says in the Bible—and by my wounds, I am healed. This is the stunning realization: the healing—in other words, the wholeness, the completeness, the home that we are really seeking—is actually right here, in the wounds, in the midst of pain, right at the heart of the very experience we are trying to escape. We are healed in the midst of everything we are running away from. We don't get healed *from* pain; we are healed, already healed, *in* our pain.

You could go even further and say that pain actually heals us. Seen for what it is, pain redirects our attention to the here and now and to the wide-open space that embraces all experience as it comes and goes. It brings our attention back to the fact that *nobody is in pain*—there is just pain appearing here in the space that I am. Thus, pain heals you from the idea that you are a victim of pain. It heals you from your illusion of control. It brings you back to this moment, your true home. It says, "I am allowed here, no matter what you think. See, I have already been allowed into what you are. I am already present. You haven't been able to resist me. But there is nothing to fear. I am only made of yourself. I cannot destroy who you truly are."

Yes, in a way that we will never comprehend, pain heals you from pain. Healing is built in to everything we are trying to escape. Sadness heals you from sadness. Fear heals you from fear. Anger heals you from anger. At the core of the most intense fear, there is nobody there who is *in* fear. Nobody there is separate from fear. Nobody there is afraid. At the center of the crucifixion, at the center of the most excruciating physical pain, there is healing. Perhaps all religions and spiritual teachings point to that truth, in the end.

This deep acceptance revolutionizes our attitude about pain, our relationship with it, our fears surrounding it. Suddenly pain, however *painful* it is, is no longer an enemy. It is a signpost pointing us back to who we really are in this moment, destroying all our false ideas about who we are. Pain is somehow *compassionate,* in the true sense of the word; it destroys all our illusions about ourselves. Nothing unreal can survive its fierce love.

PAIN AND TIME

Often what appears along with physical pain is a stressful, fearful, nervous, anxious mental reaction—an avalanche of stories about what will or will not happen in the future. I experience pain (or fear or sadness or any uncomfortable feeling) right now, but I am worried about how long the pain will last, if or when it will end, how bad it will get. Will there be pain like this for the rest of my life? Will it stay like this, or will it get worse? What if it becomes unbearable? What if it ends up killing me? What if . . . ?

The mind always seems to make things look worse than they actually are. You'll always find that your story about reality is much worse than reality itself. In reality, you only ever have to deal with *this moment* of pain. Just this moment. Just what's happening right now. In the story, you have to deal with pain in *time*. In the story, you have to deal with a whole past and future of pain! You may even convince yourself that you have to deal with a lifetime of pain, which sounds too unbearable to even think about. It is, quite literally, the mind's idea of hell. But in reality, life always spares you; it only ever gives you this moment, and you never have a *direct* experience of a lifetime of pain. In reality, there is no such thing as always or forever or never ending. Hell is a product of thought, nothing more.

Think about when you're sitting in an airplane during severe turbulence. You have a big stress reaction when you begin to imagine that the turbulence might be too much for the plane and might cause it to crash. Thought is great at telling stories of a future catastrophe. But what is the reality of the situation? The plane is going through some rough air, and as a result, you are being thrown around. That is the reality—you're being thrown around in your seat, right now. That is all that's happening. But thought lives in time, and so it says, "Well, in this moment it's okay, but in the *next* moment it won't be okay. In this moment it's bearable and I'm alive, but in the very next moment it will become unbearable and I will die. The turbulence is going to get worse and worse." And in reaction to this story, a sick feeling in the stomach, shortness of breath, tightness in the chest and throat, and heart palpitations can appear. Don't forget, the body cannot tell the difference between a real threat and an imagined threat. Great fear appears—*as if* things were about to get much worse. The body prepares itself for fight or flight—or in the case of an airplane crash, it prepares itself for death.

So there you are, sitting on the plane, preparing yourself for death, while the pilot very calmly flies the plane. He's been through turbulence like this hundreds of times, and to him, it's nothing. The real turbulence is in your thinking. In your imagination, you're flying in a plane that has already crashed! In your imagination, you're already experiencing the inevitable.

You might say, "Well, plane crashes are possible, so I'm not completely crazy!" And I would reply, "Yes, but the plane hasn't crashed yet." As long as you think it *might* happen, it hasn't happened. In this moment, your worst fear hasn't come true yet. And in this moment, it hasn't come true. And in this one. In fact, we never, ever reach that unbearable moment the mind is so terrified of. There is only the *fear of* an unbearable moment; the moment itself never comes. If things were truly unbearable, if the pain were really too much for the body, if the anger or fear were really going to overwhelm you, if the grief were really going to rip you apart, the body would go unconscious. As long as you're conscious, you're already bearing whatever is happening, even if you think or feel that it's unbearable. There is no such thing as unbearable pain. As consciousness itself, if it's happening, if it's appearing in present experience, you're bearing it, just as the ocean bears every wave, even if the wave *feels* unbearable in the moment.

You can *feel* like something's unbearable—you can *feel* like you're about to die, you can *feel* unable to cope, you can *feel* totally overwhelmed, you can *feel* hopeless and helpless in the face of things—but you can't *be* that unbearable something. As we have seen, as open space, you can't ever *be* the hopeless one, the helpless one, the overwhelmed one, for what you are is pure capacity for even the most seemingly overwhelming feeling. You can *feel* unable to cope, but what you *are* is always coping, in this moment—and there is only this moment. You can feel as if you're about to die, but what you are is very much alive. As awareness, you are already coping with what's appearing—otherwise what's appearing wouldn't be appearing. If it were truly unbearable, if life were truly unable to bear what was happening, you would not be there to know it.

This realization can remove our basic fear of life. You never reach the unbearable moment, just as the wave never really reaches the shore. The moment it reaches the shore, it is no longer a wave. That is why nobody has ever experienced death. Death is not an experience that "you" have; the wave cannot experience its own absence. Ultimately, there is nothing to fear—even if there is very intense fear appearing.

"I'm not going to make it. I can't take it. It's too much for me. It's going to kill me." These are simply passionate expressions of fear—fear that has not been deeply accepted. "It's unbearable" doesn't literally mean that you are unable to bear it; it doesn't literally mean that "someone unable to bear this" is what you really are. You *feel* unable to bear this, but that fear cannot define you. The truth is you are already bearing it, in this moment. And in this moment, which you are bearing, there is a deep fear that you can't bear it—that you don't have the strength. There is a feeling of being too weak to take this. And in the deepest acceptance, all of these waves are allowed to appear. Pain *and* the feeling of not being able to bear that pain are totally accepted here. And you are already bearing both perfectly. That's not so unbearable, is it?

In the end, you never have to face anything you cannot bear. Life doesn't give you anything you cannot handle—even the feeling of not being able to handle life. Because you are life, and life is not against you. Remember, if a wave is appearing in present experience, who you really are has already said yes to it. That's why it's here. You never have to face anything that hasn't already been allowed in. You never have to face the unacceptable. You never have to bear the truly unbearable.

It's only when you start to compare this moment with the next moment, to a future moment, that suffering begins. "This moment I'm bearing it, but the next moment I won't be able to. This moment is okay, but next moment it won't be okay. The turbulence is okay now, but in the next moment it will get much worse." We make the present turbulence *mean* so much more than it actually does.

The turbulence might get worse. But without the story that it's unbearable, without the story of this moment compared to the next one or the previous one, the deepest acceptance will still be there. The deepest acceptance is never lost, no matter what happens. What you are is *always* present. Deep acceptance will still be there, available to be discovered, even in the midst of your worst fears.

In reality, though, it's always *this* moment. The future never really arrives, does it? The future only exists as a story—and as our reaction to that story appearing now. When this awful future moment comes, it will actually be now, the present moment. The experience will happen in this space—the space that's here right now. And as this space, I know that anything that comes my way cannot destroy what I am. So let the turbulence come. I can't know it will come, and I'm not saying that I want it to, and I'm not saying I would prefer it to. But if it comes, let it come, and in the face of it, I will still know myself as the wide-open space in which life is happening. What I am is the calm at the center of the storm. I am not at war with the storm. I am the open space in which the storm is allowed to come and go. I do not fear the storm, not because I am strong and brave, but because I see the storm as myself. On the deepest level, it cannot threaten me. So let it come, if it comes.

So I no longer need to brace myself against what is to come. I can relax in the face of life and allow it all to unfold, even if that unfolding brings pain. As the space in which pain arises, I am larger than pain. I am vaster than any fear. I am so open and spacious that all of life—every thought, sound, sensation, feeling—has a place here.

In fact, bracing myself against pain has the tendency to actually amplify the pain. In trying to avoid feeling present pain, in anticipation of future pain, I tense up my whole body, which actually makes any pain feel *worse*. Avoiding pain exaggerates pain. When we relax into pain, rather than bracing ourselves against it, when we find the deepest acceptance in the midst of the pain, rather than seeing pain as an enemy, we find that healing is always very close. We can still do all we can to heal ourselves on a physical level, but, as we have seen, true healing has nothing to do with the body. The body gets thrown around, and what you are is the space in the midst of the turbulence, the ocean at peace in the midst of a raging storm, already whole, always healed.

THE VICTIM IDENTITY

Many people that I meet see themselves on some level as a victim of life. I know I spent much of my life feeling like a victim. If you have had a religious upbringing, you may have been told that your pain (or sadness, or fear, or any other feeling or emotion that feels difficult) is a punishment or trial from God, that you're being punished for being a sinner in this life or in past lives. Or perhaps you believe that you are experiencing pain because of karma, because you haven't prayed hard enough, or even worse, because you are cursed in some way. I've met many spiritual seekers who have picked up New Age beliefs that say they got ill because they weren't present enough, because they weren't positive enough, because they secretly manifested the illness for themselves, or because they didn't carry out their spiritual practices properly or follow their guru's teachings to the letter. Basically, they believe that they failed to control life in some way—that they are responsible, on a deeper level, for their present pain.

Perhaps we make up all of these stories because we don't want to face the truth: life is beyond our control. Perhaps it's easier to make up a story about our own failure to control life than to face the truth!

"If I'd just prayed hard enough, this wouldn't have happened"—you can't know that. "If I'd have been more positive, more present, more loving, this wouldn't have happened"—you can't know that. "If I'd just surrendered to my guru more totally, this wouldn't have happened"—you can't know that.

I've seen many people beating themselves up for being in pain, because of secondhand, untested concepts.

Pain and illness do tend to get in the way of our plans. We'd planned an important business meeting or a party, we'd planned to go on a retreat, we'd planned to be a success, we'd planned to travel the world, we'd planned to have fun, we'd planned to not be ill——and now we're lying in bed, incapacitated with pain. It really does feel like the illness gets in the way of "my life." It prevents me from doing what I want to do, from seeing whom I want to see, from going where I want to go. Pain cannot threaten life itself, but it appears that pain can seem like a threat to *my life*. In other words, it threatens my plans, my story about who I am, my story of who I want to be, my story of where I thought I was going, my role in the world. Perhaps all our suffering is simply a kind of grief over our dashed plans.

I have met many people who say that one of the hardest things to deal with when they are ill is the sense that they are somehow missing out on life, especially if they have to lie in bed all day. They feel disconnected from life, like a kind of outcast, unwanted. Everyone "out there in the world" is having fun, living their lives, seeking and finding what they're looking for, and here I am, cooped up in my prison cell, unable to be where I want to be, unable to continue my search. We tend to associate pain and illness with incompleteness—with feelings of being unwanted, unloved, somehow abandoned by life. Why has life done this to me? Why has it given me this pain? It must not love me. Life seems to favor the healthy, and in my illness and in my pain, I feel abandoned. It's a very old superstition.

But in truth you cannot be closer to or further away from life. You cannot be more or less alive. You cannot be abandoned by life. You *are* life, and so life *is* here even in your pain, even in your illness. You are no less whole, no less favored by life because you feel ill or there is pain. You are still this wide-open space in which everything comes and goes; no amount of pain or illness can take what you are away. In that sense, what you are cannot be ill, what you are cannot be sick, what you are cannot be broken. Only stories can be broken. Only identities can be "sick." Ideas about ourselves, ideas about what should or should not happen—those can break in two. What you are is always One.

That's the point, really—pain and illness shatter our stories about life, about control. When we suffer over pain and illness, what we are really doing is grieving over *our dreams of what should have been*. Without those ideas of what should have been, what should be now, what should be in the future, there is simply what is. The constantly changing landscape of this moment is all we ever have to face in life. And we can't know that this moment is not exactly as it should be. We can't know that things aren't meant to be exactly as they are right now. *We can't know that our lives have strayed from any kind of cosmic script.* We can't know that there is a cosmic script at all, in fact.

Beyond the story of my illness, beyond the story of my life not going the way I'd planned, beyond the shoulds and the shouldn'ts, here I am right now. Breathing. The heart beating. Sounds appearing. All sorts of thoughts, sensations, feelings dancing. Maybe some pain. Maybe some fear. Maybe the feeling of being unloved, abandoned, hopeless, weak, exhausted, lonely. Who knows which wave will arrive next? The great discovery is that it's all deeply allowed here in this space. Present experience is always being deeply accepted by what I really am, even if what's happening feels unacceptable right now. What I am has already allowed it all in. What I am has already said yes to all of it. That's why this moment is as it is. The floodgates of life are permanently open. And so when I come back to present experience, I find that this moment is never unbearable, even if I *feel* that I cannot bear it right now, just as no wave is ever unbearable to the ocean. What I am embraces all, allows all, admits all. And herein lies *the peace that passes all understanding* even in the midst of pain and illness.

Just as there is no time but the present and nothing but
the All and Everything, there is never really anything to
get, though the zest of the game is to pretend there is.
ALAN WATTS

Love, Relationships,
and Radical Honesty

Your task is not to seek for love, but merely to seek and find
all the barriers within yourself that you have built against it.

RUMI

THE ORIGIN OF RELATIONSHIP

During one of my retreats, a young woman said to me, "Jeff, all this talk of wholeness and completeness and deep acceptance and having no fixed self is really beautiful and inspiring, but what I'm really interested in is why I experience so much conflict in my *relationships*." It was a great question, and we talked for a long time about the connection between spiritual awakening and human relationships. Are relationships important, or even relevant, when it comes to waking up from the dream of separation? If there is no separate self, if I am simply the wide-open space in which life happens, are relationships as we know them even *possible?* Can open space be in a relationship with open space?

Toward the end of the retreat, the same woman came up to me and said, "Jeff, I get it now. I'm not seeking spiritual enlightenment, and I'm not looking for material wealth, or fame, or success. But now I understand that essentially I'm seeking the same thing as people who are. I'm looking for love, to find a partner who will love and complete me, who will make me feel *whole,* and I realize now that it's exactly the same seeking that drives people to live on ashrams in India or meditate for twenty hours a day or work themselves to death for that elusive promotion or sports car. I see now that we're all in this seeking game together. We all seek wholeness—we just do it in different ways. It's really humbling to admit this to myself."

For most of human history, traditional religious structures provided a real sense of security and belonging and helped us deal with the emptiness inside us. Whatever was happening, we could always turn to the Bible, the tribal elder, the priest, the rabbi, the guru, to a higher authority, for comfort, for meaning, for perspective, for wisdom. We could point to a passage in an ancient text and say, "*This* is how to live" or "*This* is what it all means." In modern times, our personal possessions, our careers, our bank accounts, the corporations, the stock markets have become our new gods. More people than ever consider themselves to be atheists, agnostics, humanists, rationalists, skeptics, secularists, or "spiritual but not religious." Many people will only believe something if it has been "proved scientifically." But science has not even come close to discovering who we really are. Every scientific answer leads to a thousand new questions. And in recent years, we also have, quite literally, *lost faith* in financial institutions, banks, corporations, and governments.

And so for many people, when it comes to a channel for their seeking energies, all they have left is romantic relationships. All the money in the world won't complete me; the church, synagogue, temple, or mosque no longer provide the release I long for; and science cannot even begin to satisfy my deepest longings. But all is not lost. I can still complete myself through another human being. I will find that special one, my other half, my mate, my companion, and I will keep them, and I will be loved and cared for, for the rest of my life, in sickness and in health. I will be whole. I will be complete. Love from another will take away the emptiness, the sense of dis-ease and lack, the longing for home that I feel deep down. Love from another will heal me from my cosmic loneliness.

Yes, we seek each other for companionship, for procreation, and for pleasure. But more than anything, we seek each other for *wholeness*. And this expectation that relationships will save us from ourselves is the cause of so much joy—and so much sorrow.

FINDING THE ONE

Turn on the radio, and the yearning of the seeker blasts out at you: "You complete me. You are always with me. I can't live without you. Without you, I'm nothing. You're the one I've been waiting for . . ." We talk about finding "the one," and indeed, that's what the seeker is always looking for—the One life beyond the myriad appearances. But can we really find this One in the form of another human being? Can another human really provide us with all the completeness we seek, all the time? Or is that really too much to ask of someone? Is that too huge a burden to place on someone else's shoulders?

I meet so many people who feel lonely, incomplete, "single" when they are not in a romantic relationship. I remember how, as I was growing up, I used to feel that there was something terribly wrong with me because I didn't have a partner, someone to "share my life with." I looked around and saw all those shiny, happy people, those totally fulfilled, loving couples, who never, ever felt lonely, and I longed for what they seemed to have. I felt like something huge was missing from my life. Ah, the voice of the seeker again! "Something's missing." Enlightenment is missing. Love is missing. Success is missing. Joy is missing. Peace is missing. The seeker lives in the world of "something's missing," the world of lack, and he looks out at the world and sees others who have what he lacks. Feelings of inferiority and jealousy can arise when we begin to compare ourselves to others.

The relationship seeker, obsessed with finding "the one," the one person who will complete them and end their search for love, moving from relationship to relationship in their quest, is like a spiritual seeker who becomes obsessed with enlightenment and follows guru after guru in their pursuit of it. But one guru after another disappoints them, until they stop and consider that perhaps their endless seeking is actually taking them *further away* from the enlightenment they long for. Perhaps it is their very search for enlightenment that is preventing them from realizing the enlightenment that is already present.

Perhaps our longing to complete ourselves *through* our relationships actually ends up detracting from the intimacy *in* those relationships. Imagine somebody who is visiting every art gallery in the world, every exhibition, every museum, in order to find the one piece of art that will complete them. They don't know what it will look like, or when or how they will find it, or how they will know that it's the one when they come across it. They only know that they have to find it. There's an urgency to their search. So they walk past painting after painting, sculpture after sculpture, and they don't really *see* what's before their eyes. They are too busy looking for "the one." All the paintings they walk past are somehow *less* than "the one." They are less beautiful, less magical, less wonderful. These other paintings simply become a means to an end. They are all somehow *incomplete* in comparison with the mystical completeness of "the one."

And of course, they never find "the one," because "the one," in manifested form, doesn't exist.

Where was "the one"? It was there in *every single painting* they walked past, ignored, dismissed, in their pursuit of finding it. "The one" was not a single painting—it was there in *all* the paintings. The one was hidden in the many. The ocean was there in *all* the waves, without exception.

You see, the love that we seek is not contained in any one person, in the same way that spiritual enlightenment is not contained in any one teacher or guru. The love we seek is *everywhere,* but our eyes are closed to it, because we are looking for it. In the Gospel of Thomas, when Jesus is asked,

"When will the Kingdom come?" he replies, "It will not come by seeking it. It will not be a matter of saying 'here it is' or 'there it is.' Rather, the Kingdom is spread out upon the earth, and men and women do not see it."

Our beloved is already spread out over the earth, and we simply do not *see*.

FALLING IN LOVE

At some time in your life, you've probably had the experience of falling in love. Suddenly, in the presence of another person (or a work of art, a flower, a piece of music, a sunset—you can fall in love in all sorts of ways), there is simply wonder, fascination, awe. Past and future fall away, the illusion of time collapses, and there is only what is—and it's an unspeakable miracle. You really see who and what is in front of you. It feels like you've finally found what you were looking for. What you were always seeking is right here in front of you. It feels like coming home, as if something in you has eventually come to rest.

But in truth, you didn't *find* love. Nobody has ever *found* love—as if love were something you could lose in the first place! You didn't really *find* what you were looking for. What really happened was that, for a moment, *your search for love fell away*. The seeker didn't find love—the seeker disappeared! The search came to rest. You briefly stopped looking for love, and the love that was always there revealed itself. Suddenly, there was no seeker, and no time in which to seek. Suddenly, there was nobody there separate from life. There was simply life, in all its mystery, wonder, and timeless simplicity.

Love is as good a word as any for what remains when the separation between us and others dissolves. *Love* points to the intimacy at the heart of present experience, an intimacy that is always there, but so rarely noticed.

The illusion of separation begins when thought says, "I love you." In other words, I, a separate person, love you, another separate person. You provide the love that I was seeking. You complete my search for love. You *are* the end of my search. It's overwhelming to be in the presence of someone who *embodies* the end of your seeking like that. It's like being face to face with God. No wonder when you're in love you go weak at the knees in the presence of your lover or your spiritual guru. No wonder sometimes you feel overwhelmed by them. No wonder it feels like they have such a strange power over you. You're unconsciously projecting onto them a power they do not have.

"I" don't fall in love with "you." It's the illusion of "I" and "you" that falls away—and that *is* love. That's why we call it *falling* in love; the illusion of separation *falls,* and what's left is the love that has always been present, but apparently overlooked in our search for something more.

No two people have ever fallen in love. Love is the death of "two." It is the falling away of the illusion of separation.

The moment I believe that anyone can complete me, I begin to want to hold onto them, to possess them, to own them, to keep them with me. When I forget the love that is always here, the love that I am in my essence, and fall into the illusion that love is somehow contained in another person, I then want to make them "mine." You can probably trace most *conflict* in relationships down to this basic illusion of possession: "You belong to *me*. You are *mine*. *My* girlfriend. *My* boyfriend. *My* husband. *My* wife. *My* partner. *My* friend. And I need you to stay mine. Because who would I be without you?"

Does anyone really have the power to *complete* you? Does anyone else contain the wholeness you seek? Can anyone really *give* you love? Or is the love that you seek from another, in reality, the love—the deep acceptance—that you are? Are you really looking for yourself, in a million different ways?

In reality, can anyone really be *mine?* Can you really *own* another person? Does the word *mine* refer to anything real, to anything other than a thought story appearing in the moment? Of course, there is nothing wrong with believing that somebody is yours and that they complete you. It's a beautiful story to tell and to keep telling, if that brings you joy. But here's the problem: When you are trying to keep hold of someone, you will inevitably begin to manipulate them in subtle and not-so-subtle ways. When you are seeking love, or approval, acceptance, praise, or even understanding from another human being, no matter who they are, you inevitably begin to say and do things to please, influence, and control them; to win them over; to keep them in your life; to prevent them from leaving you. And it all stems from your fear of loss, and ultimately your fear of being alone and incomplete again. Pain is always the result of this manipulation, both for you and for the one you are trying to control.

In our seeking, in our attempt to hold on to those we love, our love becomes conditional. We forget that love is unconditional in its nature, just as the ocean is unconditional in its embrace of waves. We forget who we really are and start seeking love outside of ourselves. We forget that love is never the result of manipulation. It can never be lost, or gained—it simply *is*.

You may not be seeking enlightenment or wealth or fame or success, but how are you holding onto, manipulating, or trying to change other human beings in your search for love? How is your seeking causing conflict in your most intimate relationships? How are you holding back from really expressing yourself in the presence of people that you care about, out of fear of rejection or of losing them totally? It is likely that if you experience conflict in your intimate personal relationships you may be looking for something that the other person cannot give you. Let's look deeper.

POWER GAMES

There are many courses, books, self-help gurus, relationship therapists, and life coaches trying to teach you how to have better, happier, longer-lasting, more enriching, and, most importantly, more *honest* relationships. But until we can understand what is happening on the most basic level in a relationship, until we can understand the mechanism of seeking, and until we can identify the dynamic that causes our dishonesty and disconnection in the first place, we will not be able to be truly honest. We will simply *pretend* to be honest. I want to take a look at what true honesty really is and how it relates to our seeking.

When asked what is most important in relationships, many people will say honesty. Telling people what you really think and how you really feel, being authentic, vulnerable, and deeply human in your interactions is considered to be the healthiest way to live. I would like to argue that when we are seeking, we cannot be truly honest, no matter how hard we try.

You want to tell the truth, to admit what is really true for you, to your partner, your friend, your mother, your father? Wonderful. But as long as you are seeking something from them—whether it's love, approval, acceptance, or security—or you simply want them to think well of you, there is always fear involved, fear of loss. To put it simply, as long as you are seeking, you are always playing a little game with them and with yourself, even if you don't realize it. *You are secretly adapting your behavior, changing what you say, hiding what you really feel, being careful, in order to ensure that they keep giving you what you want.* You hide what you really think, what you really feel, in order not to lose them and, thus, not to lose the possibility of becoming complete. You start performing, rather than relating. You relate as an image to another image, rather than as open space to open space—and your relationships can end up feeling totally incomplete and unsatisfying.

This sounds like quite a dramatic thing to say, and you might respond, "No, no, that sounds too exaggerated. I don't think I'm seeking completeness from my partner. I'm not acting—I'm just being myself!" But this seeking can happen in very subtle ways. It can be there even when you aren't aware of it. The point is, we don't *directly* experience our search for love. We simply experience the *side effects* of the search—that is, tension in relationships, dishonesty, anger, or frustration toward our partner, the nagging feeling that the other person is not who you want them to be or who you think they should be. Often seeking is experienced as a feeling of *disconnection*—from others, from life itself. The truth is, if you are experiencing conflict in your relationships, you are likely *seeking* something from your partner—or friend or parent or sister or child or boss or therapist or teacher—without being aware of it. Getting honest about what you are seeking is always the key. And this honesty always begins and ends with you.

Seeking *always* leads to conflict of some sort, because in the end, you are looking for something someone else cannot give you. Unconsciously giving someone the power to complete you is the beginning of all the trouble. *Nobody* has the power to complete you. For the power that you are really looking for—the power of completeness, communion, intimacy—does not reside in someone else. The communion you really seek is communion with life itself. What you really long for is a deep intimacy with your own experience—the deepest acceptance of every thought, every sensation, every feeling. And that cannot come from outside of yourself.

What you really long for, on the deepest level, is your-self—not yourself as in the mind-made thought story you tell about yourself, but yourself as the wide-open space that holds all life, yourself as in your true self, who you are beyond the story. What you seek is what you already are. And not seeing this, you go out into the world and seek that completeness in *another* person.

Once you've given someone else the power to complete you—once you've given away your own power (though ulti-mately it's not even your own, but this is a helpful way of talking about it, for now)—you've *also,* unconsciously, given them the power to *take the completion away,* at any moment.

If you complete me, you can also remove that completion, at any moment. If you have the power to give me love, you also have the power to take away love. This is the game we start to play with others.

The moment you give someone the power to give and withdraw love from you—the moment you make them into a guru (every seeker has some kind of guru as I will explain later)—on some level, you begin to fear them because they now have the power to make you incomplete again, to reject you, to make you feel unloved and unacceptable, to make you feel like nothing, at the drop of a hat. So you begin to feel the need to be *careful* around them. Don't upset them, or they will withdraw completion. Don't talk about this, don't mention that, tiptoe around this, pretend that never happened, don't express yourself too freely, tell them what they want to hear, be careful to say the right thing. Or, you begin to feel the need to control them, to have power over them. Through displays of your strength, intelligence, sexiness, and superiority, you will keep them with you. Either way, whether your seeking expresses itself as passivity or dominance, as inferiority or superiority, the aim is the same: don't reveal yourself too *completely*. Hold back. Stop admitting what's really true for you, and start holding up an *image of yourself* in order to please them, pacify them, or control them. Stop admitting who you are, and live out of what you are not.

This power dynamic begins to explain why many people experience so much drama in their relationships, drama that can seemingly burst out of nowhere. How quickly "I love you! You complete me!" can turn into "That's it! I hate you! I'm leaving you!"—sometimes in the space of a few moments. Peace can become war in the blink of an eye. What's going on? Are people really so irrational and volatile in their nature, or is there something deeper going on? Why do relationships so easily become a battleground, where two people are fighting for their own lives?

It's said that we hurt the ones we love. We do so because we are *seeking* so much from "the ones we love," and we are so terribly hurt when they do not provide, or when they withdraw the love we expect from them. The love of your life can become your greatest enemy so quickly. In our most intimate relationships, we can feel the greatest pain. It makes sense that intimacy and pain always seem to go hand in hand. It is those from whom we are seeking the most that seem to have the power to hurt us the most. But in our seeking, we unconsciously give them that power. They have no such power until it is bestowed upon them. In our seeking, we make others powerful in our world, and then we become slaves to that power.

Love that is conditional, love that is based on seeking, on possession, on me getting what I want and trying not to lose what I have, can easily turn to frustration, aggression, and even emotional or physical violence. When I'm not getting what I want, when I'm deprived of what I believe I need to complete myself, conflict results. This kind of conditional love will never provide what I truly long for.

Is there a love that is not conditional? Is there a love that does not depend on me getting what I want from you? Is there a love so radically open that it wants nothing in return? A love that is not afraid of being hurt? A love that never needs you to change? A love that loves you as you are, in this moment? A love that goes beyond our images of ourselves?

RELATIONSHIP CONFLICT AS AN INVITATION

As the spiritual teacher Ram Dass remarked, "If you think you're enlightened, go spend a week with your family." Those you are close to, those with whom you have a long and complicated history, are bound to bring up in you all of those little waves of experience that are not being fully accepted in your present experience—in other words, waves that are not being seen as part of the ocean. Waves that are not seen as already being deeply accepted will inevitably be brought to the surface in an intimate relationship. Your parents will bring up waves in you that may not have surfaced since childhood, waves you may have been avoiding your whole life. Your boss or your work colleagues will inevitably push your buttons about images of your competence and skill. Your spiritual teacher will force you to confront false or outdated images of yourself that you are still holding onto and defending. *People will always confront you with your own rejected waves.* And you may not like what you see, what you feel. So you will probably confront them back. And then the fun and games begin.

No matter how enlightened or awakened or free from the self you think you are, no matter how tightly you are clinging onto an image of yourself as "free from the ego" or "free from seeking" or "totally liberated and at peace," in close relationships, you are *bound* to come up against those waves of experience that are not being accepted, that are not being *loved.* It's often said that relationship is simply a mirror in which you see yourself.

Even the most so-called enlightened people may still experience conflict in their intimate personal relationships. Does this mean they are not really enlightened? Or does it mean we need to totally revise our idea of what it means to be enlightened?

When it comes to awakening to who you really are, relationships are where the rubber hits the road, no doubt about it.

Realizing that intimate relationships are always going to bring up rejected and unloved waves, one response would be to say, "I don't want to experience those waves. I'm going to avoid relationship altogether! I'm going to become a spiritual ascetic and go live in a cave in some far-off place and stay away from all people. I'm going to become celibate, repress intimate feelings, shut myself off from others. People cause suffering, and I don't want to suffer." However, this avoidance of relationship is actually a certain kind of relationship: it's a relationship in which you are *withdrawn* from other people, probably because you don't want to be confronted with those aspects of yourself you haven't allowed in. The anti-relationship relationship is very much a relationship. It's a stance toward other people, a way of relating to them that probably stems from fear of rejection.

So in the end, you cannot *avoid* relationship. You are *always* relating to others and to the world, whether you like it or not. You are always in relationship with everything—the sun, the sea, the trees, the sky, animals, thoughts, feelings, sounds, smells, chairs, tables, other people. You are the world, and the world is you, as Krishnamurti said. You are the nothing that allows everything to be.

I remember years ago, when I was a very serious spiritual seeker, I believed that I was enlightened—that I had no self, that I was nobody. I was very much attached to absolutist nondual concepts such as "There is no me" and "There are no others." I used to believe that all relationship was an illusion—that anybody in a relationship was deluded and stuck in the dream of separation. If there is no self, how can there be relationship? Who would "nobody" have a relationship with? If there is no me and no you, how can there be any kind of relating whatsoever? Back then, whenever somebody said, "I love you," I would secretly laugh at their delusion. And so I went through a period of withdrawal from the world, and I thought that was enlightenment. I disengaged from life, and I felt free—for a while.

I realize now that the way I was living had nothing to do with enlightenment. I was simply lost in my concepts *about* enlightenment. It wasn't that I actually was nobody and, therefore, couldn't have relationships; it's that I was *scared*, terrified even, of real, intimate human relationships. I was terrified of exposing myself in all my nakedness and rawness to another human being. Why? Because unconsciously, I feared that someone would see through my façade, that they would see through the false image I had created and call me out on the fraud that I was. "There's nobody here" and "There are no others" are beautiful pointers to the ultimate truth of existence, but the seeker will easily hijack those pointers and turn them into rigid beliefs, using those beliefs to *avoid* real, honest, authentic human relationships in the here and now.

No wonder I retreated into my enlightenment cave and avoided intimate human relationships. I was scared of being found out. On some level, I knew that all images I was holding of myself were fake—including the image that I had no image of myself! I was terrified of being exposed, of being seen for the fraud that I was. I was afraid of losing my image of myself as some transcendent nonentity and being a human being again!

The end of seeking is not a cold, inhuman detachment from life, from others, from relationships, although this may be a stage that some people go through in their journey. The end of seeking is the possibility of real, brutally honest, authentic human relationships, because when there is no seeking, when you are no longer looking to another human being to complete you, when you no longer need to manipulate others for your own benefit, when you no longer see separation, you are finally freed up to really listen to others, to really meet them where they are, to really see and hear and understand who and what is there in front of you. The end of seeking opens up a huge space where you can really be honest in your relationships, without having to hide behind spiritual concepts such as "There's no me" or "Relationship is illusion"—or behind any concepts, in fact. All concepts burn up in the fire of real life, in the furnace of intimacy. In recognizing who you really are, you are free to truly love the one in front of you without fear, without defensiveness. Love is seen to be truly unconditional in its nature.

All our beautiful spiritual insights about wholeness and the nonexistence of the seeker are wonderful, but if those insights don't extend right into the most intimate parts of our lives, if they don't reach right down into the depths of our personal experience, if they don't lead to the extinguishing of seeking in all its manifestations, they remain simply words. Believing that you have no self or that you are "nobody" or that everything is Oneness is all wonderful, but what happens to those insights when your partner, or your son or daughter, or your mother or father bursts into tears because he or she is upset with something you just said? Do you just dismiss them because they are "lost in a dualistic story"? Do you tell them to leave you alone, because there's "nobody here"? Do you tell them they need to become enlightened like you, and then they won't suffer? Do you withdraw from them and force them to go off and meditate, or self-enquire, or work on themselves, until they calm down and see clearly? Do you give them a lecture on how there is no such thing as relationship, and if they think there is, they "still have an ego"?

Or are you open—really open—to *listening* to what they have to say, and finding the deepest acceptance in your own experience while listening? When you're no longer seeking anything from them, when there is no self-image to defend, when you recognize yourself as open space, is there not the space to simply listen? Is there not the space to see the world through their eyes, to find out in which ways what they are saying might be true, to find the place where you actually see eye-to-eye? And is there not also the space to be really honest about how you feel in response and to allow them to have their own response to that, even if it's not the one that you'd hoped for—even if it ruins your dreams, hopes, and plans; even if it destroys your precious image of yourself, the one you have been protecting your whole life? Is it possible to stay open, no matter what?

OUR MUTUAL NAKEDNESS

I feel that a lot of spiritual teachings do not recognize the direct connection between seeking and inauthenticity in relationships. You can claim to be enlightened, free from separation, free from all seeking, but what does all of that mean if, behind the scenes, you are still in desperate conflict with your wife, your children, your boss, your parents, your loved ones, your students? It would be easy to excuse all of this conflict by saying something along the lines of, "Even after seeking ends, these imperfections carry on. They're just the impersonal functioning of the character, just the part prescribed by life, by the cosmic movie script, by destiny," and so on. But understanding the mechanism of seeking, you can see that this is like saying, "I'm no longer seeking, but I'm still seeking."

The end of seeking and honest, clear, fearless communication go hand in hand. In fact, I would say it's impossible to write a book about deep acceptance and the end of seeking without including a large section on honest speaking and listening. Whenever you're being emotionally dishonest with someone, whenever you're hiding how you really feel in the moment, whenever you're trying to hide a part of your experience in order to hold up an image, whenever you're playing a role with someone rather than being honest about what's really happening for you right now, the likelihood is that you're seeking something from them. *You want them to see you in a certain way.* You are trying to manipulate their image of you (which is actually your image of their image of you). And in their presence you want to see yourself in a certain way. And what else could be the reason for this but fear?

We try to protect ourselves from life and from each other because we are afraid, and what the seeker fears more than anything is being exposed. Exposure of the seeker is like death. To put this in simple language, if you saw me for who I really am, in all my weakness, failure, insecurities, incompleteness, you would reject me. If you saw me in all my rawness, in all my nakedness and humanness, without the masks I wear, stripped of my façade, without defenses, without the games I play—if you saw what's really here, if you saw beyond the image—*you'd reject me*. If you saw my fear, my frustrations, my doubts, my sadness, my feelings of failure, ugliness, incompetence, helplessness, you would not love me. Or, if you loved me before, when the image is gone you would soon lose that love for me. I fear that in the light of truth, in the light of life, all the little games I play would be exposed, and I would be left standing there, naked and ashamed, unloved and abandoned, *an outcast, far from home*.

The fear of being an outcast seems to go very deep in the human psyche. An *outcast* is literally someone who is *cast out* of a tribe, expelled from a social group or community, sent away from their village, their home, to die in the forest, in the wilderness, with nobody to protect them. The fear of being an outcast is the fear of being cold and alone, unprotected, forgotten, vulnerable, and near to death.

Although we may no longer fear being torn apart by wild animals in the forest, we still somehow unconsciously associate social rejection with a kind of death. If I expose myself to you, I might *die*. That's how it feels. Being an outcast is a deeply not-okay wave in the human ocean. And so we spend much of our lives avoiding intimacy—and instead pursuing more superficial goals such as popularity, fame, or just fitting into the crowd. When I was in college, I remember there was one student whom everyone loved. He always had a group of friends around him, no matter where he went. Back then, I assumed that, with all of that company, he must be the happiest guy of all—the most whole, the most complete, the most fulfilled. I was a little in awe of him, a little scared of him, and a little jealous. On our graduation day, I spoke to him, and he told me how lonely he felt, how lonely he had always felt, even though everybody knew him. "Everyone knows me, but nobody really *knows* me. I know so many people, but I feel so isolated," he said before he gulped down another beer.

You can be surrounded by people and still be lonely. Your life can be full of dinner parties, family get-togethers, social occasions, nights out, conferences, retreats, meetings, workshops, and festivals, and you can still feel totally disconnected. You can find your perfect partner and the two of you can be the perfect couple, the couple who everyone thinks will live happily ever after, and you can feel more isolated and lonely, and probably more confused, than you ever were before. No matter how many relationships we have, no matter how full our lives are with people and possessions, if there is no deep *connection*, no real honesty, no intimacy in the true sense of the word, you simply will not feel fulfilled. There will still be something missing. There will still be emptiness and a sense of lack.

And then, even with all the promises in the world, you will always be haunted by the risk of losing love. Even with all the external security in the world, even with all the vows and commitments and the most seemingly solid future plans, you will feel insecure in your relationships. The only true security is radical honesty in the here and now, which means risking the loss of your self-image and fearlessly meeting the other as yourself, undefended and unprotected.

OUR STORIES ABOUT EACH OTHER

Do you ever really know another person?

We talk about "other people"—falling in love with them, being in relationship with them, being in conflict with them, ending relationship with them, meeting them, under-standing them, having and losing them—but do we ever really directly experience others as outside ourselves? Or is our experience of other people always inseparable from our *own* stories—our *own* thoughts, beliefs, assumptions, projec-tions, prejudices—about them? Are "others" really "other" to us? Are they really separate from what we are?

Just as we never really experience an outside world—a world outside of present experience, as we have seen—do we ever really experience other people as "out there"? When we relate to someone, who are we actually relating *to?* Are we simply relat-ing to an *image* we have created of them, rather than to who they really are in the moment, here and now? Do we end up missing others as they are in this moment in our attempt to hold onto our own story of them, our own *version* of who they are? Do we always view others through the filters of history and future, and miss what is *present?*

Who is your friend, partner, mother, father, brother, sister, when you see them without your story about who they are—without your story about what they believe or don't believe, who and what they love or don't love, what they've done and haven't done, what they've said or haven't said, how they've hurt you or praised you or ignored you—in the story of your life? What if you were to meet, here and now, beyond all of that carryover from the past? What if you were to meet them, here, for the first time, without expectation or disappointment or even hope? What if you were to meet the one who is *actually here,* rather than the one whom you imagine is here?

What would it mean to meet—really meet—without history, without projection, without imagination?

Now, I'm not for one moment suggesting that we get rid of our stories about each other; I'm not suggesting that we forget about the past, about the details of each other's lives, our names, our roles, and so on. I'm suggesting that when we live solely in our stories of each other, we end up missing what's actually here right now. In clinging tightly to my story of you; in holding tightly to memories, to prejudices, to my conditioned ideas of who you are; in viewing you as a separate character moving through time, I miss you as you are now, in this moment. I miss the one who is actually in front of me. I am so locked into a past image of you, into my ideas of who you are, into my expectations of you, into my disappointments and fears, that I don't really *see* you as you are. I don't really *hear* what you are saying right now. I value the past over your present-moment experience of the world. *It's as if I already know who you are, what you are going to say, what you are thinking, what you will do, what you believe, what you want, before you even open your mouth.* I have literally prejudged your experience. All prejudice begins here.

I remember several years ago when I walked into the kitchen and saw my father for the first time. Of course, it wasn't literally the first time I'd seen him—I'd seen him thousands of times before—but this was the first time I'd really *seen* him. It was the first time I saw what was actually there—not what I imagined to be there, not what I hoped to be there, not what I thought should be there, but what was actually in front of my eyes. I saw beyond the story "He's my father" and beyond the story "I'm his son," and what I saw was, well, simply what was *there*—an elderly gentleman with gray-white hair, sitting at the kitchen table, eating some cornflakes.

Who was this man? I had to admit, really admit, the truth—I didn't actually know. All of those years of "knowing" him, all of those years of certainty about who he was, and I had never really *met* him. I had been too enmeshed in my father-son-relationship story to really see the one who was actually there. In all of those years spent trying to be a son, trying to play that role in the way I thought it should be played, trying to hold up that false identity, trying to relate to him as a father, with all the conditioning and expectations that word brought with it, I had missed the reality. I had called him "my father," and I had assumed I knew what I meant by that. But could those words, *my father,* ever begin to capture who and what was actually here? Could this man ever really be mine at all? Could anyone be mine? Without the story, who was I, in this moment, in relation to this man?

Beyond the story, there was only *intimacy* with the one in front of me.

Somehow it was *in* that not knowing that we really met. Beyond the roles; beyond the "father" story, the "son" story; beyond the concepts of how a father should behave, what he should and shouldn't be able to give his son; beyond the conditioned ideas of what a son should expect from his father; beyond our history, we really met. Past and future were stripped away, and all we had together was now. *This* was the only moment. How precious it was—and how precious he was, how fragile, how mysterious. How *fascinating* he was too. I saw the wrinkles on his hands, the lines on his face, the little bit of saliva dribbling down his cheek. His hands trembled a little as he lifted the spoon to his mouth. His fine, white hair stood up a little in the back. His breathing was a little raspy.

It was almost like being in love. He was a work of art.

Stripped of the story—the story of expectations, the story of what I needed him to be, the story of how he had or hadn't been the father I needed, wanted, expected, or had been promised—how *innocent* he was. I had made him *guilty* by expecting so much from him, by seeking from him something he could never give. I had placed a burden on his shoulders— the burden of being "Father," the burden of being the one to complete "Son." In my seeking, in my search for home, in my need to hold up an image of myself as "Son," I had held him up as "Father," with all the expectations that word brought. We had never truly met each other.

But he could never live up to my image of "Father," the image that had been programmed into me. Nobody can live up to an image. In comparison with this "father" image, he would always be imperfect. He would be too this or too that—too emotionally withdrawn, too concerned with money, too closed minded, too unspiritual. Too involved in my life or not involved enough. Too father or not father enough.

But without the image, there was an undeniable perfection here. He wasn't too this or too that. He was just as he was, in this moment. And nothing else was *possible* but this moment.

It was bittersweet, this meeting. It was intimate and beautiful, but it was also a kind of loss. A loss of the roles, of "father" and of "son." A loss of the past and the future. A loss of time itself. And all that was left was a timeless love with no name, both radically impersonal and intimately personal at the same time. Words will never even begin to capture it, this mystery at the heart of the most ordinary of things—the mystery of a man eating cornflakes at the breakfast table. It's enough to break your heart, over and over again for the rest of your life.

I still carry on calling him "my father," of course, but underneath, it's known that he could never be mine. I cannot own him—or anyone. I wouldn't want to own him; possession destroys intimacy. But somehow—and here's the paradox and mystery—in that loss, in that death of possession, I actually lost nothing. All that was lost was *illusion*. All that was lost was the dream that the one in front of me could ever match my image of him, could ever be what I expected him to be.

The idea of our father-and-son relationship had actually gotten in the way of present-moment relating with the man in front of me. In holding up the story of our relationship, the story of father and son in space and time, we had stopped *seeing each other in the here and now. In our relationship, we had stopped relating.*

Beyond the story of "us," beyond the dream, beyond all our images of each other—that is where true relating is really possible. Beyond the father story, the son story, the mother story, the daughter story, the husband story, the girlfriend story, the student story, the teacher story—that is where true intimacy lies. And the reality is, we *always* meet beyond the story. We always meet beyond the image. What I am, what you are, is the open space in which all images come and go. What I am, what you are, cannot be defined by any story. As consciousness, I am what you are, always. I am what you are, and that is unconditional love.

When I relate to you as separate self to separate self, as one story to another, in a sense, there is no true intimacy. I play a role, and you play a role. I play son, and you play father, with all the expectations and demands implied by those words. I play daughter, and you play mother. I play sister, and you play brother. I play guru, and you play disciple. I play "me," and you play "you." I identify myself as a role and then try to relate to you, another role. I adhere to my script, and you adhere to yours.

But when I relate to you not as a separate self, but as the wide-open space in which all thoughts, feelings, sensations arise and fall away—that's where real intimacy is possible. We meet, without a history, open space to open space, and that's the beginning of real relationship—not the relationship of one story to another story, not the meeting of two images, but the meeting of two open fields of being, open fields in which all thoughts, stories, feelings, sounds, sensations are deeply allowed to come and go. (And there aren't really two open fields coming together, but this is useful language for the time being. Ultimately, no language can capture this intimacy. All language is only temporary, in this place beyond words.)

As a story trying to complete itself through you, seeking resolution through you, trying to come home through you, I will end up manipulating you, being dishonest with you, playing a role with you, hiding how I really feel out of fear of losing you, punishing you when I feel hurt by you. But as open space, I am free to communicate honestly and authentically with you, knowing that I am already the love I seek; knowing that I do not need you to complete me; knowing that, deep down, I cannot ever lose you. I do not *need* you in order to be fully who I am. I do not need you to keep my story together.

In recognizing myself as the open space in which all thoughts and feelings are allowed to come and go, and in recognizing that what I am is beyond "son" and that what I am doesn't need "father" to complete it, *I am free to engage honestly and authentically with the man in front of me.* I can allow him to be fully himself, to express himself freely. I can encourage him to explore, to express his true thoughts and feelings, because finally I do not see his experience as a threat to my identity. Ultimately, even if he leaves me, it does not detract from my completeness.

It is the most loving thing in the world to say to someone, "I don't need you. I love you, but I don't need you." In other words, "I don't need you to complete me. I am complete without you. But I enjoy your company right now, and I love being around you. And if you were to leave, I would still be able to love you—even if there was pain or sadness in the experience of that."

Real love asks nothing in return.

TAKING ANOTHER'S PERSPECTIVE

> *And if I only could*
> *I'd make a deal with God*
> *and I'd get him to swap our places . . .*
> KATE BUSH, "Running Up That Hill"

A man had been sitting quietly in the front row during one of my meetings. At the end of the day, as everyone was leaving to go home, he came up to me. He was red faced, sweating profusely, and quaking with rage. He had bulging, unblinking eyes. He came up a few inches away from my face and told me, in no uncertain terms, that I was a fake, a phony, a fraud, and a liar; that I was dangerous; that I was misleading people; and that I needed to wake up immediately—or else. He told me that I was responsible for all the evil in the world, that I was a reincarnation of Hitler, that I needed to take full responsibility for what I had done to the world. He told me that he was fully enlightened and had come to wake me up, and all I needed to do was submit to him. It was my last chance to awaken, he said.

"You have dreamt of this moment, haven't you, Jeff? You're afraid of me, aren't you?"

Now, you can imagine how easy it would have been to make him wrong, to tell him that he was crazy, to physically remove him from the room, to attack him back, to become a guru and try to prove my own strength and superiority, to demonstrate the advanced level of my spiritual evolution. In response to that kind of anger, that kind of threat, it would be tempting to reject him totally. He had rejected everything about me—my entire teaching, my entire existence. And more than that, he had come to save me from myself and wanted me to submit to him!

But I was intent on engaging with him in a deeply human way. Had he really just come to attack me? Or was something else going on? Despite everything, I wanted to find the place where we could meet. As the vast ocean of consciousness in which all waves are already accepted, there is always a place where I can meet another beyond the story, even if that place seems far off. Where could I meet this man? How could I see through his eyes, when his eyes seemed to be seeing things in such a distorted way?

I remained honest with him. I told him that no, I wasn't afraid of him but didn't particularly want to participate in his staring contest. (He refused to blink and interpreted my blinking as fear, as a clear sign that I wasn't enlightened, like him.) I explained to him that he had misinterpreted my message—that I wasn't simply saying, "There is only Oneness" or "There are no people" in the way he assumed I was. No, I hadn't dreamt of him, but I was interested in what he had to say. No, I didn't feel like I needed to wake up or that I was misleading people, but I was eager to understand why he was so angry with me. I too had once been very angry with spiritual teachers. I understood his anger. Perhaps we could meet there. I tried to take his position, to see through his eyes, to find out how he had come to his conclusions. I wanted to look past his "enlightened guru" performance and find out what was really going on for him. What was he seeking? What did he really want? What was he truly longing for?

I encouraged him to explain, clarify, and I gave honest responses that weren't attacks on him, but gentle, firm statements about my own experience. I didn't presume to know anything about his experience—I could only report on my own. We can never truly know another's experience. As I stayed there, engaging with him, trying to find a place where we could truly meet, something strange happened. Because

I wasn't rejecting him, withdrawing from him, or reacting to his anger, because I did not fear him, because I was simply being myself in the true sense of the word, recognizing the deepest acceptance within my own experience, he began to relax a little. He wasn't being met with attack, but with understanding, and his guard started to drop.

As we talked, I realized that he had not come to attack me at all. He had come to try to make me agree with his opinions—he had come to be heard. I had the feeling that this was a man whom nobody ever listened to, although he made the most noise (it's often that way). His point, which he was making in the most roundabout way imaginable, was that teachings of Oneness could easily be an excuse for people to stop taking responsibility for their lives. The idea "there are no individuals" was false to him, because he saw a world where people were suffering, and he refused to allow anyone to deny that relative reality. He didn't want people to transcend the world; he wanted people to be part of it, to engage fully with it, rather than escape into spirituality, and he had come to wake people up from their dream of transcendence. He had assumed that I was just another Advaita teacher denying relative reality—perhaps that's what he had meant when he had called me Hitler. He thought that I saw myself as above humanity, and calling me Hitler was a brilliant way of trying to bring me back down to earth! As I clarified my position, as I asked him questions about himself, as I listened to him and found the places where I actually agreed with him, or at least saw the truth in what he was saying, he relaxed. I knew I had nothing to defend. His whole body started to slump.

Yes, I agree that nonduality can easily be used to deny relative reality. *Yes,* on one level, personal responsibility is very important. *Yes,* I am a human being like you. *Yes,* I agree, it's important not to mislead people. *Yes,* I can see how I would be a fraud if I believed in a false image of myself as a spiritual teacher who had all the answers.

It was very strange. I found myself agreeing with him in some ways—with a man who only ten minutes ago had called me the devil and rejected my entire message. He became quieter and quieter. He asked for some of my water. His mouth was dry. I handed him my glass. He looked like a little boy, lost. We sat in silence for a while. He started to open up about his own life, to reveal personal details about himself. He told me that it was his life's mission to visit every nonduality teacher (and he saw me as one) on the planet and wake them all up! He told me that I was the first nonduality teacher he had ever visited who had not verbally insulted him or had him thrown out of the room. I found it quite funny, even endearing, that this man spent his life trying to wake up nonduality teachers from the dream of nonduality. I found some respect for the rebel in him, since I found it in myself. We even had a little laugh together, we rebels.

On his way out, I don't know why, but I felt like giving him a hug. He warned, "Don't hug me, Jeff. It's dangerous." I suddenly saw a little boy whom nobody ever hugged and who came to the conclusion that he must be dangerous and unhuggable. I hugged him anyway. Hugging is never dangerous, in my experience.

I felt compassion for this man who had something very intelligent, and even important, to say, but simply did not know how to say it without resorting to threatening people and hiding behind an image of himself as an enlightened guru. He felt that he had to play at being the savior of mankind, driving everyone around him away, rather than engaging on a human level with people, talking things through, allowing others in, making his point in a way that people could hear. That would be too intimate, too honest, too human, too truthful, too dangerous! To truly meet in intimacy would destroy all his images of himself. I can understand that too; I used to live daily in that place of fear and disconnection and spiritual superiority.

He was clearly his own worst enemy. He longed to be heard—and underneath that, loved, as we all do—but the way in which he communicated made it virtually impossible for people to hear him, love him, or even stand to be in the same room as him. As a result of his inability to communicate, he had been rejected time and time again, by some of the most "enlightened" teachers in the world. I refused to play this game with him (and anyway, rejecting him would just be rejecting a part of myself), and, instead, met the human being behind the mask.

I am not telling this story to make myself out as a saint. I am far from that. I wanted to show how common ground can be found even in the most frightening and confrontational encounters, and how it is possible to meet those who reject you (threaten your image of yourself) on every level. Because I recognize myself as the wide-open space of awareness in which all images and feelings are allowed to come and go, because I am not holding up a specific image of myself as a nonduality guru or a teacher with all the answers, because I know that uncertainty, doubt, and even failure are deeply allowed into my experience, I did not feel the need to defend myself from his attack on nonduality teachers. And so because I was listening from beyond the image, I was free to hear what he was really saying. And more than that—I was free to find the truth in what he was saying.

I didn't *agree* with everything he said—not at all. And I certainly don't *condone* the way he speaks to people or his threats of violence. And perhaps I would ask for him to be kept from entering any of my meetings in the future; that might be the intelligent, and most compassionate, thing to do. From this place of deep acceptance, we are always free to take practical steps to intelligently resolve a situation.

But that's not the point; the point is that, despite everything, we found a place to meet. He left not as an enemy. Our meeting ended in a clean way—nothing was left unresolved. We found our inseparability; we found the place where we were not at war. I found him in myself.

When you really listen to someone, when you really listen to their perspective, their viewpoint, their expression of their experience of life, their story about what they have noticed in their world, you can always find some truth in what they are saying, however challenging, confronting, strange, extreme, and absurd their views seem at first. It doesn't mean you agree with them. It doesn't mean you condone their behavior. It doesn't mean they become your best friend, and the two of you go out for beers every weekend. It just means you find the nugget of truth in what they are saying—and that, in the moment, is the end of psychological conflict. I have never met anyone whom I couldn't meet on some level, however much I disagreed with what they were saying, however much they sought to destroy me (as in the story of "me"). In recognizing who I really am, I see that there is no thought, no feeling, no emotion that is alien to me on the deepest level, just as there is no wave that is alien to the ocean, and that is why there is always a place to connect, even with people who seem totally out of reach. As the philosopher Ken Wilber says, "Nobody is capable of producing 100-percent error—nobody is smart enough to be wrong all the time."

There is no thought you can have that I can't have. There is nothing you can feel that I can't feel. You are not fundamentally different from me—it's not possible. All of human consciousness passes through us, and so we can always meet somewhere—even if it takes a while to find that place.

You see, in a very mysterious way, your thoughts are my thoughts. Your feelings are my feelings. Any thought, any feeling is part of the river of human consciousness that flows through the open space that I am, that you are. In that sense, no aspect of human consciousness is unreachable, alien, inhuman. If you are a human being, I can meet you somewhere, even if it's a struggle at first to find that meeting place where we connect, the place where we are no longer at war. Even if I have to access parts of myself that I'd rather cast out.

This is what it really means to find common ground with someone. The ground that is common to us is the ground of awareness. We meet there and share our perspectives. There, in that place, there is no need to agree or disagree; there is only to listen and see and feel the truth in what the other person is saying—even if, in the end, you don't agree with them. I love what Voltaire said: "I disapprove of what you say, but I will defend to the death your right to say it."

The end of war always lies in finding our common ground— the ground of awareness.

And who knows? I may even learn something from the one I previously called an enemy. My enemy can be my greatest teacher, because in bringing up discomfort in me, he also brings me into contact with the image of myself that I'm still defending. In other words, he shows me which parts of my own experience I'm still at war with. He shows me the waves that I'm not allowing into my ocean. He reflects back at me the enemy within, so to speak—the parts of my own experience that I have made into an enemy by not seeing their inherent completeness. He is my greatest teacher, shining the light on my rejected waves, although he probably doesn't realize this.

My enemy wakes me up from my dream of image identification.

Now, this deepest acceptance of another's experience doesn't mean you become a total pushover. I can hear the objections now: "Jeff Foster is saying we should just agree with everyone, let everyone get away with anything. That would lead to total chaos and destruction!" No—not at all. This acceptance doesn't mean that you always make yourself wrong and you always make others right. Deep acceptance does not equal passivity. It doesn't mean hiding your perspective or pretending you don't have one just to appear kind or spiritual or nonjudgmental. (The biggest judgment of all is that all judgments are bad!) From this place of deep acceptance, I can respond to your experience authentically and with passion. But it's no longer coming from a place of "How dare you say or think that!" It's no longer coming from a place where I'm withdrawing love, where I'm mentally punishing you for thinking or feeling the way you do, and where I'm making you wrong. It's no longer a reaction, an automatic defense of a threatened image of myself. It's a response in the true sense of the word. I am simply responding to this moment as it appears, to life as it is, rather than to life as I thought or hoped or expected it to be. I am responding to what is actually happening now, from a place of deep acceptance, without seeking anything through that response. This is true responsibility (response ability)—the ability to respond from beyond the image. The end of conflict lies not in reactivity, but in this total responsibility, which emerges from the discovery of the deepest acceptance of this moment.

"Love your enemies," as Jesus taught. In other words, let your enemy wake you up from your dream that you have an enemy in the first place. Ask your enemy to show you what false image of yourself you are still defending.

THE FORGIVENESS OF EVIL

You could say we are all looking for love—the saint and the sinner alike. We just have different ways of expressing that search. The man who confronted me at my meeting may have seemed like he wanted to tear down the "Jeff Foster" image, but what he really wanted was love. The alcoholic wants another beer, but what he really wants is love. He feels uncomfortable in his present experience—unloved in every thought, sensation, and feeling—and seeks a way out, and the only thing that seems to alleviate that discomfort is beer. Beer, for a while, seems to remove the not okay and bring the okay. Beer, for a while, seems to bring the womb. Even the serial killer, the rapist, the murderer are all looking for the womb, in their different ways. We are all womb-seekers on legs.

For some people, the only way they know how to get love is to hurt others. For those who feel completely powerless, helpless, beaten down by life, and long to feel powerful and in control again, hurting or even killing seems to provide some temporary release. Yes, the seeker can become desperate in his or her quest for wholeness. We'll take wholeness in any way we can. We'll fight for it. We'll die for it. We'll blow ourselves up, if we have to, to reach heaven, to come home, to release the burden of separation. For some people, the only path they can find that will take them home is a path littered with enemies. *You become my mortal enemy when I perceive you as blocking my path home.*

This is why human beings go to war with each other, not only to win or defend land, food, or material riches, but also over differences in viewpoints, philosophies, ideologies, religious beliefs. So very quickly do differences of opinion between people—be they two people in a relationship or the citizens of two countries—turn into holy wars. When you disagree with me, when you reject my viewpoint, I feel *threatened* in some way. Strange, isn't it? You're not threatening me physically, but I still feel like I'm under some kind of attack. Why? What is really being attacked here?

When I am holding onto an idea, belief system, or ideology, and have made that belief system my path to wholeness—my only path to wholeness—and you suggest, by your words or actions, that my belief system is wrong, you are threatening my wholeness. You are blocking my way home. You are threatening my life—as in the story of my life. *We don't argue over ideologies; we argue over our paths to wholeness.* The wave is trying to return to the ocean, and if anything blocks that, the wave is confronted with the most terrible possibility: That it will never, ever come home. That it will always be separate. And so it will use extreme measures to wipe out this threat. Some people blow themselves up—and try to blow you up—just to validate their own journey home.

Deep down, even suicide bombers are simply trying to come home, like anyone else. How, *without condoning their actions in any way,* can we even begin to have a shred of compassion for people like suicide bombers? Discovering the homesick seeker behind the suicide bomber is where we may begin. This is not about condoning violence—not at all—but understanding where the urge for violence may come from, in them *and* in us. Perhaps when we really understand what's going on, we will be in a much better position to deal with the reality of the violence in the world—not adding to it, but helping to unravel it at its very source. When we finally go beyond the story of "them and us," when we finally go beyond the illusion of good and evil and the underlying illusion that we are separate people, perhaps we have a chance.

Realizing that basically every single human being is trying to come home gives us a whole new way of understanding the behavior of people that we call violent, crazy, sick, or evil. Seen in this light, nobody is really inherently evil, nobody is fundamentally different from us. Some people just *seek wholeness in desperate ways, and the destructive actions that come out of this desperate seeking we call "evil."*

Those we label as "evil" are essentially looking for what we all are looking for, but because of their unique conditioning, what they learned and experienced growing up, the way they were treated as children, the cards they were dealt in life, the only way they can find wholeness right now is through violence. Not feeling deeply complete in their present experience, not experiencing the love inherent in the present moment, they become desperate seekers of love, and in that search for love, they go to war with the world. In their search for completeness, they end up destroying everything that they perceived as incompleteness "out there," in the world.

All that we see as evil in ourselves, all of those waves of experience that are not deeply allowed to arise and fall, all of those waves that are a threat to our self-image, we will project onto our so-called enemies out there in the world. In trying to hurt or wipe out our enemies, we are secretly trying to wipe out the evil in ourselves. In trying to destroy impurity in others, we are really seeking our own purity. In trying to destroy the dark in others, we are secretly seeking the light. I want to destroy incompleteness in you because I secretly want to destroy it in myself and become complete.

Our enemies become our scapegoats. The seeker always has a *scapegoat*—a word that has an interesting origin. In ancient tribes, when villagers wanted to rid themselves of sin, they would sacrifice a goat to the gods. They believed that the goat would magically absorb their sins, and when the goat was killed, their sins would die with it, leaving them clean again. Scapegoating is a way of trying to make our-selves psychologically clean—in other words, trying to free ourselves from "dirty," unloved waves. In our seeking, we create scapegoats all the time. We continually look outside of ourselves for release, and in extreme cases, we may even try to destroy others in order to destroy parts of ourselves we don't want to live with.

What I do not allow in myself, I will not allow in you. The waves I want to get rid of in myself, I try to get rid of in *you*. Adolf Hitler—often spoken of as one of the most evil people of all time—gave us a classic example of this scapegoating. He persecuted homosexuals, and yet there is strong evidence to suggest that he was deeply at war with homosexual urges in himself. He accused his enemies, the Jews, of being sexually unclean, and yet there is evidence to suggest that he secretly enjoyed very "unclean" sexual fetishes. He said Jews' blood was poisonous and contagious, and yet evidence shows that in his youth, he was terrified that his *own* blood was poisonous. Did Hitler honestly believe that destroying his enemies would give him what he truly longed for? It's incredible, this projection game—how simple it is and yet how much destruction it causes when it is allowed to run rampant on a global scale. We have the whole of human history to show how scapegoating does not actually lead to peace in any sense of the word. Our enemies can never really be destroyed, for they are in us. Separation begins with me and you, here in this room, and it ends with torture and genocide.

And how easy this mechanism is to see in others! Can we see it in ourselves? That is the question. Who are your scapegoats? What do you reject in others that you secretly reject in yourself? Weakness? Failure? Fear? Homosexuality? Violence? What thoughts and feelings do you not admit in yourself, in order to hold up to the world an image of who you are?

Now I want to say here that none of this is about condoning unkind, violent, or destructive behavior. I am simply suggesting that we look deeper and discover where that behavior is coming from. Someone who is deeply at peace with their own experience, someone who recognizes the deepest acceptance in every thought, sensation, feeling—is this person really going to feel the need to lash out at the world? Is this person really going to need to seek release in a dramatic and extreme way? Is someone who sees that every aspect of their experience—every thought, every sound, every sensation, every feeling—is already deeply embraced, deeply accepted by life, really going to need to go on a desperate hunt for completeness? Are they really going to need to destroy the world around them in order to find that completeness? Is hurting others really going to give them what they long for?

When you see that another human being is, in essence, yourself, is it really going to give you any satisfaction to *intentionally* hurt them? When you are no longer defending a false image of yourself (an image that you know cannot even begin to capture who you really are), when you are no longer seeing another human being as a threat to that image, are you really going to feel the need to attack them? Is violence really necessary when you no longer fear the one in front of you?

I imagine that violent, destructive, or intentionally unkind behavior is *always* an expression of seeking within someone's experience. Violence and conflict begin as seeking in my own experience, and then get projected out into the world.

Think of all the times in the past when you've done or said something mean, unkind, cruel, or violent. Be honest—where was the urge to hurt someone coming from? Was it coming from a place where you were clearly seeing that everything in your present experience was deeply okay? Were you recognizing the deepest acceptance within your own present experience? Or was it coming from a hurt place, a feeling of not being okay in the moment, a place where you felt the need to lash out in order to feel okay again and prove yourself? And did lashing out really lead to you feeling okay, in the end? Or was the relief only temporary? Did *guilt* appear afterwards—in other words, had you pretended to be something you were not?

Seen from this perspective, we could say that the world simply becomes a blank canvas on which to play out our seeking activities. If I am at war with my own experience, I will go to war—in various ways, some subtle and some not-so-subtle—with the external world. Of course, ultimately what we call "internal" and what we call "external" are not really separate; the world and I are one. The urge for violence comes from *not seeing* this intimacy between myself and the world—*not seeing* that, as open space, I am essentially insepa-rable from what you are. It comes from *not seeing* the inherent okayness and completeness of every wave of experience. In seeing parts of myself as evil, I go to war with that same evil in the world, in my desperate attempt to reach wholeness. Unconsciously, I am only trying to destroy the evil in myself. "Evil people"—dictators, murderers, rapists, serial killers, ter-rorists—are really trying to make the world whole again, to make themselves whole again, in the only way they know how. However strange it sounds, "evil people" are actually trying to *destroy* evil—the evil in themselves. So let us not create more evil by going to war with them, and let us not condone their behavior either. But let us come to *understand* them on a deeper level than we've ever done before, by seeing our inseparability from them. Who knows? Perhaps then an end to evil is truly possible.

Realizing the true nature of evil is when true forgiveness can begin. When Jesus was being crucified, he looked down at his tormentors and forgave them. Forgiveness is possible when you see that people are not violent and aggressive and intolerant of your position because they are evil, but because they are simply seeking and perceive no other way to find what they are looking for. They do not *see* wholeness, and therefore, they go out into the world and *seek* wholeness, by destroying everything they see as a threat to wholeness, everything they think is responsible for things not being whole. In not seeing wholeness, they go out and destroy their scapegoats.

Dying on the cross, Jesus said, "Father forgive them, for they know not what they do." In other words, "Forgive my enemies—they don't *see*. They are ignorant of wholeness. They are ignoring who they really are. They don't see the ocean in the waves. They have identified themselves as separate people. And so they are innocently playing out their seeking. They think that killing me will bring them wholeness, and it won't. For they are already whole, but do not realize that. Killing me a thousand times won't bring them what they really long for. Because what they really long for is who I really am—who they really are. I am what they are. Maybe one day they will see."

Who would you rather be—Jesus, who knew who he really was and recognized deep acceptance in his own experience, or his torturers, ignorant of their true nature, totally identified as false images, and deeply at war with themselves? Who would you rather be, the perpetrator or the victim? And who is the real victim—the one who hurts others because of deeply unaccepted pain or the one who experiences pain but knows who he really is within that experience? Who is truly hurt here?

It is interesting to note that the word *forgiven* literally means "given everything." In seeing that, in this moment, completeness is given—in other words, in seeing that in this moment, in spite of what is happening or has happened, in spite of what someone may have done or said to me, I am still whole, and this present experience is deeply accepted—the other person is relieved of the burden of guilt, so to speak. They are no longer an enemy; they are no longer responsible for my loss of completeness. Another wave cannot take away your completeness. Another wave cannot make you more or less ocean. Nobody can take deep acceptance away from you. On this level, everyone is innocent. And so, forgiveness is no longer a question of *trying* to forgive others. It's about seeing that, in this place of deep acceptance, everybody is already forgiven. Everybody, including you, is already given everything. Forgiveness is built in to who you are. Nothing real can be taken away from you. And, as the *Course in Miracles* reminds us, nothing unreal exists.

FORGIVING OUR GURUS: THE END OF SEEKING ACCEPTANCE OUTSIDE OF OURSELVES

When the one in front of you is relieved of their burdens—the burden of having to be the one to complete you and the burden of being the one who can threaten your completeness—they are relieved of their guru status, stripped of their imagined completion power. And when this happens, finally you can see them for who they really are. The power struggle is then over, and a true, authentic human meeting is really possible.

When I'm no longer transferring my seeking needs onto you, I am free to see you in your incompleteness too. I can see you as you are. I can see your human flaws, your failings, your weakness, your sadness, your pain. I can finally love you for who you are, not who I thought you were or who I needed you to be. I can love you in your pain, in your grief, in your imperfections, in all your humanity. Beyond the roles, beyond the stories, your imperfections are so perfect.

If the seeker places a burden of expectations on their guru, they also burden themselves with those expectations. Because when we are seeking something from someone—whether they be a lover, a friend, a therapist, a parent, a spiritual teacher or guru, or even a politician, celebrity, or leader—we give them a power they never had. And we feel bound to that power, bound to them in some way, tied down and unable to walk away freely. They seem to exert some strange, mystifying power over us.

The seeker is always bound by what they seek. They feel unable to walk away from their guru, the one they believe will complete them. People spend decades hanging around their spiritual gurus, waiting to get something, really and truly believing that the guru has something that they don't. By focusing on the guru and waiting for the guru's transmission or revelation, they lose trust in their *own* experience. They are constantly waiting for validation, living off someone else's authority. Even when the guru is abusive—verbally, physically, or emotionally—the seeker still stays there, desperately trying to silence their own doubts, desperately clinging onto the hope that it will all be worth it in the end and they'll get what they came for.

A man once told me that, in his early twenties, he came across a photo of an Indian man in a friend's living room. Until this point, he'd not been into spirituality; he knew nothing about spiritual paths, and he had never seen the man in the photo before. But—as the man described to me—in the moment of seeing the photo, something very strange happened. It was almost as if energy were emanating from the photo. There was a kind of power there, a presence. It was so magnetic, so *attractive*. In that moment, the man in the photo became his guru, and he set off to India to find him.

The man said to me, "It's so strange. *I wasn't looking for anything at the time.* I wasn't seeking enlightenment at all. The power just *emanated* from the photo. It had nothing to do with me. It was all there, in the photo. Here, take a look."

He showed me the photo—he still carried a tattered copy in his wallet. It was a beautiful photo, for sure. The guru looked very serene, happy, at peace, in that moment. I'm sure this guru had some beautiful insights to share. But power? I didn't feel any power emanating from the photo. I didn't feel more or less drawn to this man than I do to anyone else. He was not fundamentally different from what I am. He was simply another beautiful wave in this cosmic ocean, a piece of music that was different, but not fundamentally different, from all the other music. When you're not seeking, you see what's really there, without the projections.

What this man carrying the photo described was a perfect example of the seeking mechanism at work. He claimed that he wasn't seeking anything when he encountered the photo. But *every* individual is a seeker, even if they don't realize it. Every wave seeks the ocean. This man may not have been seeking enlightenment specifically, but he was a seeker of love, of completeness, of deep acceptance. And he thought he had finally found what he was looking for in the form of the Indian man in the photo.

Everybody is just seeking unconditional love. Not getting it from our parents, our partners, or our careers, we then go looking for it in the form of a spiritual guru or healer.

Most of the time we don't *realize* we are seeking anything. We simply find ourselves drawn to people, bound to people, apparently sucked in by their energy, by their strange power. We feel compelled to drop everything and travel to India to go see a man in a loincloth. We go weak at the knees when a celebrity walks into the room. We faint when we meet our idols in the flesh. We submit to powerful leaders; we do exactly what they tell us. We put all our critical thinking and intelligence and gut instinct on hold to please them. We swoon when our beloved walks into the room, and we do everything to please her, to keep her happy, to win her favor, even when it feels inauthentic to do so. The seeker is overwhelmed by the object of their seeking. But this experience of external power is always our own projection, based on a misunderstanding of who we really are.

The band Everything But The Girl recorded a song called "I Didn't Know I Was Looking for Love Until I Found You." This is exactly the point: I didn't know I was looking for love until I found you, and suddenly you became the end of my search for love. I didn't know I was looking for enlightenment until I found a photo of an Indian man, and suddenly I projected the end of my search onto him. But the lover has no power until we give them that power, and the guru has no power until we project that onto them. The power of search-completion, which we call "enlightenment" or "love," or even "fame" or "genius" or "power," is projected onto the person, and we forget that it's all our projection, not a power that anybody, in reality, can really have. So then we go off into the world in search of that power, to get closer to it, to touch it, to attain it, to absorb it, and then to prevent ourselves from losing it.

Everyone wants to be close to the guru. Everyone wants to be near the celebrity. Everyone wants to touch the garb of the saint, the pope, the spiritual leader. We find ourselves strangely drawn to these people, and we don't know why. We just blurt things out like, "They're amazing! They are so present. They have this energy. They radiate something. They are so otherworldly . . ."

They walk into the room, and we faint; we are really fainting at our own projection. They walk past us, and we feel their energy; it is our own energy, projected. They stare into our eyes, and it feels like they are "transmitting presence";

you are, quite literally, experiencing yourself, your own presence. When we experience power as coming from outside ourselves, it really is our own power, projected. In reality, there is no inside and outside power; there is only life power, which has no inside and outside. There is no inside and outside of the ocean; all is water. There is no inside and outside of this moment.

Once, at a conference, a seeker of enlightenment told me he had experienced energy emanating from me. He said he had "felt my presence" from across a hallway. Understanding the seeking mechanism, I could instantly see what was going on. In his search for enlightenment, he had projected his image of an enlightened being onto me (he had to, as a seeker). So to him, I appeared to have a power; I appeared to radiate presence, to leave a trail of energy behind me wherever I went.

Now, I know that I do not radiate. I do not leave trails of energy. I am not special in any way, nor do I have the power to complete anyone. And if I believed this about myself, how arrogant I would be! But I did not invalidate this man's experience. Instead, I gently reminded him that it was his own energy, his own power, his own presence that he was seeing "out there." He was holding "the end of seeking" outside of himself, in order to keep his seeking going. It was his own waking dream—no different, in essence, from the dreams he had at night.

Now, there's nothing wrong with being drawn to someone because you believe that they have the power to complete you, enlighten you, take away your pain. But the shadow side of this is obvious: *We lose our own power.* We lose faith in who and what we are. We stop trusting our own deepest experience. And then we start being dishonest with ourselves and with others. We stop seeing them as human beings and start treating them like gods. We start being careful around them. We tiptoe around, trying to say the right things, feel the right feelings in their presence, so as not to be rejected, shut out of the club. We fear them as much as we love them. We try to impress them, to win their favor. And we feel lost without them. We need to be around them to get our "kick." We start living secondhand lives, always waiting for other people to make us feel complete in our present experience, living off the authority of others. We are seeking the deepest acceptance everywhere except the only place it can be found—here and now.

I have met people who have been abused by gurus or cult leaders, and they put up with the abuse *although on some level they knew what the guru was doing was wrong.* They lived in the hope that the guru knew what he was doing, that it was all for their own good, that eventually it would all lead to their enlightenment. They repressed or silenced their doubts, because they were told that all doubts, all disagreement with the guru, any criticism of his methods were signs of weakness, of fear, of ego.

Why didn't they walk away from the situation? They couldn't—they were seeking. The seeker can't just walk away from an abusive situation—there's too much at stake. However much you're hurting me, I need your love. I need your enlightenment. I need your approval. I fear its loss. This is the dark side of the projection game: we lose our common sense; we ignore our discernment; we repress our intelligence; we ignore our gut feelings and intuition; we silence our doubts, many of which may be valid—all in the pursuit of our own completeness. We end up going against our own present-moment truth in search of an abstract truth in the future.

In our seeking, we always lose faith in our own present-moment experience, and so we end up seeking that faith outside of ourselves. We begin to live in hope of a future salvation that never comes.

I've found that often people's anger toward their abusive guru (or parent or partner) dies down when they realize that, in reality, they *always* had the freedom to walk away. They just *felt* like they couldn't because they were seeking something. The guru didn't really take away their freedom—they took it away from themselves, because they were seeking something from the guru. When they were no longer seeking anything, they could see the guru as he (or she) was—a human being with some beautiful insights to share, but trapped in his identity as an "enlightened, ego-free being," at war with the world, raging against other peoples egos, unable to see his own raging ego. The god becomes a human being again, and the seeker is freed. Truth always frees. *Only* truth frees.

I love what Krishnamurti says: "If you do not follow somebody, you feel very lonely. Be lonely then. Why are you frightened of being alone? Because you are faced with your-self *as you are* and you find that you are empty, dull, stupid, ugly, guilty, and anxious—a petty, shoddy, secondhand entity. Face the fact; look at it, do not run away from it. The moment you run away fear begins."

We follow others, we look to them to complete us, because *we cannot face our own incompleteness*. We hope that another— a lover, a guru, a bottle of vodka—will take our incompleteness away. Letting go of the guru means letting go of the hope of escape that they promise and facing ourselves as we are. And that means facing all of those waves in ourselves that we reject, the waves we see as dark or evil or deadly. Great fear can arise at this prospect.

But really it's the most beautiful thing in the world to realize that nobody can be who you need or want them to be for you. Nobody has the power to complete you. Nobody can do that for you. Nobody can *be* that for you.

Everybody is innocent of being unable to provide the completeness you need. The gurus are liberated from having to provide what they could never provide. And you are left here, liberated from their power, liberated from the need to mindlessly follow them, facing your present experience, which is the real guru. Yes, present experience is the guru that will never promise you anything it cannot deliver; it will never lead you astray, disappoint you, hurt you, abuse you, and it will never, ever leave you. It does not need your approval, and you do not need to fight for its love. It is ever present and free.

In seeing beyond the story, everyone is *forgiven*, in the true sense of the word. All of those people who disappointed you because they didn't live up to your expectations of them are forgiven—father, mother, sister, brother, friend, lover, spiritual teacher. They couldn't complete you; they were too busy trying to complete themselves. They were being themselves perfectly. They were not being what you needed perfectly. They were not completing you perfectly. *And thank goodness they never completed you,* because they brought you back to the realization that nobody can complete you, which brought you back to the possibility that maybe nobody can complete you because you are already complete.

All that is left is gratitude—for the people you love, for the people you can't stand being around, for the people who bore you to death, for everyone who has ever entered into your life, for everyone who has ever exited. Everybody is playing their roles perfectly. They enter right on cue; they exit right on cue. The play is perfectly choreographed. And it's all one giant invitation to see through the seeking mechanism and come home—to see, to really *see,* what's there, beyond what you imagine is there, beyond what you dream is there, beyond what you think should or should not be there. You can imagine that the universe breathes a sigh of relief every time the true reality of the present moment is recognized.

So now it's no longer two seekers in a relationship, two waves trying to reach the ocean through each other. It's no longer two people using each other to complete themselves. It's no longer a tug of war, a battle of self-images. Now it's two people who see each other as they really are, who see each other in all their failings, insecurities, and flaws, and who are no longer trying to fix each other, to make each other match the perfect-partner image—the "perfect partner" who was supposed to complete me. Now it's two people who see clearly what's in front of them.

Two people who can finally be honest, in the true meaning of the word. To be honest means "to tell the truth without expectation," without aiming for a particular result, without trying to hurt or manipulate the other person in any way. Honesty means telling the truth and being *willing* to experience everything that follows. It means telling the truth not with the aim of changing or fixing the other person, but simply because the truth is what I long for the most. What I long for the most is to let go of the burden of trying to hold up a false image of myself in your presence. In the end, we don't need a reason to tell to the truth, to admit what is. Truth is its own reward.

TELLING THE TRUTH OF THIS MOMENT

We are now in a position to take a closer look at what honest communication looks like and how simple it is when you are no longer seeking—in other words, when you have noticed deep acceptance in the moment and are, therefore, no longer waiting for acceptance, validation, or love from another. Honest communication is the easiest thing in the world when you are willing to be a failed seeker—when you are willing to experience *everything in this moment;* when you are willing to deeply allow all the waves that appear now, however uncomfortable they may be; when you are willing to give up relationship (as in the *story* of relationship) and truly *relate* in the moment; when you are willing to lose the image and be who you really are.

I once met a woman whose husband was quite ill, and although she loved him very much and cared for him deeply, she felt uncertain as to whether she wanted to go on being his wife after many years of his infidelity. He was in a lot of physical pain, and although she felt a deep compassion for him, on another level, she felt things could not go on the way they were in terms of their romantic relationship. She was very confused about what to do. She was torn between kindness and honesty. She didn't want to hurt her husband, but at the same time, she could no longer go on hiding how she felt. She was spending sleepless nights trying to work it all out.

This woman had been a spiritual seeker for her whole life, and one of the things she had picked up on the spiritual path was that it was important to *accept* everything. She was trying desperately to accept her husband as he was, including his infidelity, but she just couldn't, however hard she tried. She was experiencing a lot of anger for the way he'd treated her over the years. On a deeper level, she felt hurt, betrayed, and unloved by him. (Much of our hurt is simply a variation of our feeling unloved.) And for many years, she had been putting her life on hold, *waiting* to be loved by him, *waiting* to be accepted, *waiting* for him to apologize fully and transform and become the person she had always wanted him to be. She had spent her whole life living with a dream of him, living in hope, and the hopeful dream was starting to die.

The truth was, in this moment, despite all her beautiful spiritual insights over the years, she could not accept her husband. This nonacceptance was a huge blow to her spiritual identity. As a veteran spiritual seeker, she felt that there was something *wrong* with her for not being able to accept the situation by now. She had failed to accept both herself and her husband. She was a failed seeker, and that failure was very hard to admit. When she saw me, this woman was on the edge of a total mental collapse.

The acceptance she was really looking for would not come through *trying* to accept (she'd been doing that for years), and it would never come through *seeking* acceptance from her husband (she might wait for the rest of her life for that). The acceptance she was really seeking was the deepest acceptance— the acceptance that she was, in her essence, the wide-open space of awareness that already accepts all thoughts and feelings as they come and go. She was asking her husband for something he could never provide, and because he had not provided it, her frustration, anger, and disappointment with him had grown to unbearable levels.

The question to ask yourself is always this: *what is my truth in this moment?* In other words, *what do I really think and feel right now? Can I simply admit what is appearing in present experience? Can I begin to admit these thoughts, these sensations, these feelings, however much I don't want to admit them, however much they threaten my image of myself? Can it then be seen that what I admit is already admitted into present experience? Can it simply be noticed, right now, that these waves have already been allowed into the ocean—that what I am has already said yes to this moment, that the acceptance I seek is already here?*

If I am to truly accept this moment, as many spiritual teachings tell me to do, I must accept *everything*—simply everything—that's appearing right now. And that everything could include any *resistance* or *nonacceptance* that is appearing right now. From the point of view of the ocean, *all* waves are accepted, including all the ones we don't like or want in this moment. Acceptance doesn't have to look or feel pretty. True acceptance goes beyond all our ideas of what acceptance should look like. True acceptance is what you are in your essence—it is that which allows this moment to be exactly as it is. Even the unacceptable is accepted by what you are. This acceptance is radical.

Remember:

To *admit* what's appearing in present experience—in other words, to simply and effortlessly notice that these thoughts, these sensations, these feelings are present here and now—is to notice that these thoughts, sensations, and feelings have already been *admitted* into this moment by what you are, even if you don't want to *admit* that, because it threatens an image of yourself!

So, in this moment, what is my truth? My truth is that I cannot accept this moment. I admit that, even if it threatens my image of myself. I think I should be able to accept; I know spiritual teachings tell me to accept. But my truth, in this moment, is that I cannot accept. That's what is. I must tell the truth. I must *admit* the nonacceptance.

In this moment, I'm unable to accept my husband, my wife, my friend, my boss, my mother, my father, my guru. In this moment, I'm unable to accept their behavior, what they said to me, what they did to me. In this moment, I'm unable to accept them as they are. Maybe tomorrow I'll be able to. Maybe next year. Maybe never. I don't know. All I know is that, right now, I cannot accept. I admit the truth about this moment. I admit what is.

The real freedom comes in seeing that my present nonacceptance of them is totally acceptable to life, in this moment. I *admit* the nonacceptance (or pain or fear or sadness or anger or boredom or whatever is appearing now) and discover that it is already *admitted* into present experience. It's what is, and it is held by life in this moment. That's the real acceptance I've been seeking—an acceptance that's deeper than any acceptance you could offer me, deeper than any acceptance I could find in the world of time and space.

When I'm no longer seeking your acceptance, what is there to fear in being honest with you? I won't lose acceptance. Even if you reject what I say, even if you cannot hear it right now, even if you disagree totally, I won't lose this acceptance. This acceptance will even be there if I experience any rejection from you. It holds me, always, even in the midst of conflict.

And so, out of the recognition that my truth is totally accepted by what I am, in this total admitting of present experience, *I am now free to tell it to you without fear*. My truth might be difficult for you to hear, but it is my truth, and I cannot apologize for that. I cannot apologize for the waves that are already deeply accepted in this ocean. I am not in control of this deep acceptance. I am not in control of the ocean.

So the woman may have found herself saying something to her husband like, "It makes me sad to see you in so much pain. I do love you. But right now, I just cannot accept our relationship as it is." It would be an honest, loving, powerful statement, said without fear. It would be a statement of fact—not a threat, not an insult, not an attempt to manipulate, because she was not afraid of losing acceptance.

Once you see what's going on in your experience, once you see the seeking that's happening and are honest with yourself about it, communication becomes effortless. There is no longer any need to work out how to communicate. Communicating becomes a matter of simply *saying what you see*. It is telling the truth about what's really going on for you, in your experience—without expectation. What could be simpler than that? Clear and honest communication flows naturally from the realization of deep acceptance of present experience.

I asked the woman, "What would you say to your husband if you were no longer fearful of his response—or trying to manipulate him or waiting for him to accept you, to love you, or even to apologize?" She told me that, besides feeling great love for him, she also couldn't deny that she had the urge to hurt him, to punish him in some way for what he'd done to her. And underneath that, she could feel deep sadness and disappointment—that he hadn't been the husband she'd expected, that he hadn't been the one to complete her, that she couldn't *control* how he felt for her. At the very bottom, she found a sense of loss and feelings of helplessness in the face of life, as we all do when we sit with our suffering long enough and let it reveal its secrets.

Without the deepest acceptance of her present experience, she would quickly identify herself as "the unloved one" or "the helpless one" or "the failed wife" and go to war with her husband. But in deepest acceptance, there was no longer any need for these stories. Deep acceptance always destroys our false stories. The pain, the sadness, the disappointment, the helplessness were all *embraced*. They were *admitted*.

Admitting these feelings didn't feel very spiritual or loving or kind, and it destroyed the woman's image of herself as a highly spiritually evolved being. But it was her truth, in that moment. When we drop all ideas of what this moment should look or feel like, we are free to admit the truth. It is the truth that frees us from the burden of living as an image. Communication is then as simple as *putting this present moment into words.*

"Right now, I feel sad and disappointed with you and with myself. I can't deny that there is some anger here too. I know that I *don't* want to hurt you, but I can't deny that there is anger here. At the same time, I feel sad that you are in so much pain right now, and sad that our relationship hasn't worked out as I'd hoped and dreamed. But I still feel great love for you in this moment. And I'm not asking for you to change—I'm really not. I just wanted to be honest with you about how I feel today. I want to stop pretending to be something I'm not. I've been waiting for years for you to give me something that you could never give me."

It might not feel kind to say such things, but this woman had reached a point where things couldn't carry on the way they were. And she couldn't wait for her husband to be the one to change. Things had become stagnant; feelings had bottled up inside her, and the only way to break through was to be totally honest. All the woman would be doing was saying *everything*, without apology and without expectation. She would be admitting the truth of the moment. The unconditional *yes* that you are allows for a clear and honest expression of *no*.

I can't think of any situation where total honesty is not going to bring about a more authentic, more real relationship. Even if that honesty results in changes that are uncomfortable at first, even if it feels unkind, even if it breaks the status quo and disrupts old patterns, being honest in the way I've described cannot ever be wrong.

By saying, "I love you, *and* I cannot accept you right now," the woman would not be trying to win her husband's acceptance, his approval, his love. She would not be holding back or attacking out of fear of losing his love or acceptance. She wouldn't be pretending that everything was okay in order to hold up an image of herself as enlightened or spiritual. She would simply be stating, honestly and authentically, everything that is appearing presently in the space that she was. She would be real—as real as a human being can be in the moment.

In this way, brutal honesty becomes an expression of love in itself. Brutal honesty is never a threat to love—it *is* love. If love can be threatened by this kind of authentic, loving honesty, it isn't the kind of love you truly long for.

"I'm saying this not to hurt you, but because I love you, and I want to be honest with you. If I didn't care, I wouldn't be so brutally honest with you like this. I don't know where we go from here. I don't have the answers. I don't know what we should do. *I really don't know.* But I'm open to exploring with you."

See how there's no real effort in this *admission* of present-moment experience. There's no story I need to hold up, no image of myself I need to defend, nothing I need to work out. When I tell the truth like this, I cannot "get it wrong." It's an effortless stating of what's going on in the ocean that I am. It's a simple report about the waves that are already present, spoken without the hope of a specific outcome.

Communication is easy, but because we are seeking, it seems infinitely difficult.

This is why I always say there is no "how to" communicate. Clear, honest communication flows effortlessly from a place of deep acceptance. When you're not seeking someone's love, acceptance, or approval, you can afford to tell the truth of this moment, which is the truth of who you are. There's no risk in it. You start to see that the real risk is in not telling the truth—you risk living a life of inauthenticity, of held-backness, of disconnection and quiet desperation. You live as an image, and you feel distant from the one you love.

What a burden it is, having to carry all of these stories about ourselves, having to manipulate people to get what we want, having to play power games, having to battle each other for completeness—a completeness that never comes. How exhausting it is to not *forgive*. Much of our suffering is due to our own dishonesty and inauthenticity in relationships—not saying what we mean to say, not saying what we really feel, not saying what we really want, crafting clever and intricate stories to win people over and prevent people from leaving. It's all such a burden to carry, this split in our experience between public and private self, between who I really am and who I make myself out to be, in order to win your favor. It's a constant performance, a role that I must put so much effort in to maintaining.

The real meaning of the word *guilt* is "burden" or "debt." When you're seeking something from someone and not telling the truth about your present experience in order to get it, on some level you feel guilty. In other words, you know that one day your dishonesty will be discovered. Metaphorically speaking, the debt you owe will have to be paid. As a child and young adult, I was so inauthentic in my relationships, there was such a split between my public and private self that I used to walk around some days feeling nauseous. I was terrified my cover was about to be blown. I felt, quite literally, guilty, even though I'd done nothing "wrong."

These days, because I am no longer seeking anything from others, I am totally free to be honest with others. It's such a relief—to live without guilt. Because I love myself—in other words, I see that every aspect of my experience is allowed and embraced by life—I can communicate that experience to you honestly and without fear of rejection, without fear of losing love. And so I can love you and stay connected, even when we disagree, even when what you say or do *hurts*.

Honesty is *connection*. When I'm being truly honest with you, when I'm really telling the truth and no longer living as a façade with you, I no longer feel disconnected from you. And so, I no longer *long* for connection with you in the future, and I no longer *fear* loss of connection, because I notice that in this place of deep acceptance I am always and already connected with you.

Here, in deep acceptance, we don't have to *try* to connect via the story of our relationship, for we are already connected, beyond that story.

HEARING ANOTHER'S TRUTH

Sometimes people come up to me and say, "Jeff, I really get what you're saying—it's all about being present with what is and simply admitting what's true. But in the heat of the moment, for example when someone is unkind to me, or a colleague at work criticizes me, or my partner complains about something I've done, it all falls apart, and I forget how to allow the present moment, and I get caught up again in the dream, in my seeking."

The beauty of other people is that we cannot control them. However honest we are, however kind and loving we are, however understanding or helpful or enlightened we think we are, however deeply rooted in acceptance we appear to be, people still get upset with us. They still get angry; still misunderstand us; still want us to change; still think that we are wrong, that we aren't seeing things clearly, that we aren't living in the way we should be living. People will never stop telling us their stories, sharing with us their views of the world and of us. This is either a terrible thing ("Hell is other people," as Jean-Paul Sartre wrote in *No Exit*), or it is a real opportunity to really see what we are still at war with, which waves of our experience are still not being allowed in.

However enlightened you think you are, other people will carry on projecting their ideas of you. You have no hope of stopping this! You either go to war with them, defending your own image of yourself, or you start listening—really listening—and come to understand why they see you the way they do. Perhaps if you had seen what they had seen, heard what they had heard, experienced everything they had experienced, you would see you in the same way too. If you saw through their eyes, perhaps you would think and feel exactly the same way as they do right now. You really don't know.

It's one thing telling *your* truth—perhaps that's the easy part! The harder part is to be able to hear *someone else's* truth, to really hear their response, their perspective, or their viewpoint, especially if it's about *you,* and to find the place where that viewpoint is okay—where it's okay for them to think what they think and feel what they feel, in this moment, even if you strongly disagree with what they have to say, even if right now you do not understand how they could possibly feel the way they do.

Authentic communication has nothing to do with agreeing with everyone all the time or with making everyone right and yourself wrong. Neither of these options is realistic, and they probably stem from seeking—from a need to be liked, approved of, admired, loved. Authentic communication has everything to do with hearing—really hearing—another person's perspective, with meeting them where they are. And then, after having found that common ground, after "meeting them in their world," as I like to say, you are still completely free to make your voice heard. But you're no longer talking to them as an enemy. You're no longer in separate worlds. You meet them in their world, in their perspective, and walk with them from there.

What do you do when your partner comes in and tells you that he thought you were rude to one of his friends the other day? Or when he shares that sometimes he fantasizes about other women? Or when he says that he is annoyed with the way you don't do enough cleaning around the house? Or he tells you that you are not the woman he wants you to be? In the heat of the moment, how do you react?

The heat of the moment is where the rubber hits the road in spiritual awakening.

Here's where much conflict in relationship begins: you share something with me, and it *hurts* me on some level.

You share how you feel, how you see me; you share your viewpoint, your perspective, your belief. And it hurts me. It scares me or angers me or simply makes me feel uncomfortable or like some kind of failure. I immediately feel like I have to make you wrong, to stop you from thinking and feeling the way you do, to correct your experience, to change and control you. If I feel hurt enough by what you say, I may even feel like I want to counterattack, to hurt you as you've hurt me—perhaps in a very subtle and clever way, so it doesn't look like I'm trying to hurt you.

Or I am so hurt that I withdraw totally from you. I tell you I'm never going to speak to you again, as a way to punish you. I threaten to leave, to end the relationship. But what I really wish were over is not the relationship, but my own lack of deep acceptance *within* the relationship. What I really want to leave is the dishonesty, the façade, the holding up of images, the lack of present-moment relating. We can never really leave relationships, for we are always relating in one way or another, whether or not we tell the story that we are "in a relationship."

When you say something to me, and it hurts, and I feel rejected and unloved in that hurt, there's a temptation to run away from the hurt feeling, to not allow myself to feel it and to immediately move to defend myself by withdrawing from you or attacking you in some way. There is such a temptation to "skip a step"—in other words, to skip the step of actually feeling the hurt and deeply allowing it in, and instead, to move immediately into defense and attack. We often don't allow the hurt feeling, which can appear as a sick feeling in the stomach, a tightness in the chest, or a constricted feeling in the throat, and we try to escape it.

I feel threatened by what you are saying to me—in other words, the threat of ego-death rises up—and so I quickly move to *invalidate* your experience, to neutralize the threat. Your thoughts about me are totally wrong. Your feelings are not valid. Your point of view is crazy. "I can't believe you think that! I can't believe you feel that! How dare you! You're sick!" we say. In our rush to defend ourselves, we end up shutting off or withdrawing in some way. Defense is the first act of war, as Byron Katie reminds us.

The truth is, whether you like it or not, whether you agree with them or not, the other person *does* think and feel the way they do right now, in this moment. You may not like it, but that is their present-moment experience. They may not feel that way tomorrow; they may not feel that way in a week's time. But they do now. Can it be okay for them to experience what they experience right now? Can it be okay, just for a moment, for you to *not* correct them or make them wrong? Can it be okay for you to *feel* hurt, in this moment, and not do anything about it, however much the ego rebels against this?

Conflict ends when you can listen to someone from a nondefensive place of deep acceptance and love, a place beyond "I am right and you are wrong," a place where you fully honor and allow their present experience of life, however absurd or unkind other views may sound and feel to you. Conflict ends when you can stay open to being perceived as wrong, even if you are quite certain that you are the one who is right. Conflict ends when you stop pretending to have all the answers, and instead you listen, really listen.

What does it mean to honor someone else's experience? Can I deeply *allow* you to think what you think and feel what you feel right now? Can I *allow* you to express your experience freely and openly to me? At what point do I make what you say, what you think, and what you feel not okay? At what point do I go to war with you?

If you tell me that my hair is purple, it doesn't hurt me. I know for a fact there is no truth in what you are saying. If you tell me I'm a fool because I have five legs, it doesn't hurt, because I see the absurdity in what you're saying. But if you say something to me that threatens a real image that I'm holding of myself, well now I'm going to see some truth in what you're saying. Remember how I talked before about negative thoughts, and what happens when we try to hold up a fixed image of ourselves? Now, when that image is being threatened, there's the possibility of being hurt.

You say something to me, and I feel that I'm being attacked in some way. You tell me I'm wrong; that you were upset at something I said; that you don't see me in the way I see myself; that I'm unreliable, unintelligent, unenlightened; that I didn't do something I was supposed to. I feel hurt by what you said. I don't want to be the "unreliable one" or the "unenlightened one" or the "one who was wrong" or "the failed one." I reject those images. They are not me. They do not have a place in what I am. I cannot admit them into myself.

I feel that if you really loved me, you wouldn't say what you said. You would see me for who I really am and not believe your own story about me. I feel unloved, unwanted, unappreciated, or misunderstood by you, and almost immediately a fight-or-flight response kicks in. The poor old body doesn't really know the difference between a real threat (a tiger approaching me, baring its teeth, getting ready to attack me physically) and a psychological threat (a metaphorical, image-munching tiger approaching me, hungry to devour my images of myself). The threat of physical death and the threat of identity death—it's hard to tell the difference sometimes. We run away physically from the tiger that threatens our bodies, and we mentally run away from that which threatens our images of ourselves. What's the difference? We attack the tiger physically, and we attack the metaphorical tiger's own image of itself, trying to tear it down. What's the real difference?

Most of us are very rarely attacked physically. Most of our suffering comes from our identities being attacked, hurt, threatened, or bruised in some way, and our response to those attacks. We act *as if* we had been physically attacked. In defense of images, in defense of our precious tales of ourselves, we go to war with each other.

The question is, when you feel hurt by what someone has said to you, *why* does it hurt? *Why* do you get so angry? What are you trying to defend? What image of yourself is being threatened? What unwanted thoughts and feelings are appearing in the space that you are? Watch how quickly the urge to not feel those waves appears—along with the urge to defend or attack.

In the heat of the moment, instead of rushing to defend a threatened image of myself, can I find the place where everything that is appearing right now is deeply accepted? Can I simply view this moment as one giant invitation to deep acceptance? The feelings of being unloved, the possibility that you're right and what that says about me, the fear that you're rejecting me, even the fear that it's the end of the relationship and you will leave me—can all of this simply be here, in this moment? The tightness in the chest, the feeling that you've just been metaphorically punched in the stomach, the constricted sensation in the throat, the feeling that your whole world is temporarily falling apart—can all of these waves of experience be allowed, deeply allowed, in this moment? Forget about allowing them tomorrow; forget about whether or not you were able to allow them yesterday. Can they be allowed now? *Now* is all that matters.

Even if you have said something very challenging to me, even if I feel deeply hurt, insulted, rejected, unloved, can I discover the deepest acceptance in the midst of those feelings? Can I simply allow myself to *feel* hurt, to *feel* pain, to *feel* sadness, to *feel* anger, to *feel* unloved, to *feel* helpless and powerless in your presence, and not do anything about it, just for a moment? Can I allow that hurt fully into myself, just for a moment? Can I find the place where the hurt is already allowed?

When we fully allow ourselves to *feel* hurt—however much that admission goes against our common sense and threatens our egoic sense of pride—we stop being hurt. In other words, hurt, deeply accepted, destroys the story that I am "the hurt one."

Relationship conflict begins when hurt is *not* deeply allowed, and I move into the story of myself as the hurt one, the victim of hurt. As the hurt one I will inevitably make you into "the one who hurt me," and I will inevitably begin to punish you in some way—to attack you or in some other way defend myself against your threat. As your victim, I will begin to fear you.

When deeply accepted, pain and hurt are not the *end* of relationship. Instead they become *part* of relationship. They can even bring us to greater intimacy. We can find the place where we can love each other even in our mutual pain. Deeply accepted, pain is not the end of our love. It does not oppose our love. It is allowed *into* our love. Our love is vast enough to hold any amount of hurt, any intensity of pain. And so we continue to relate, to stay together, even in the presence of hurt.

Yes, here is the key to breaking through all relationship conflict: *if I want to stay connected with you in this moment, I must deeply allow any hurt that appears.* This goes against all our conditioning, which tells us to protect ourselves *against* hurt. But the place where I shut off from the hurt, the place where I do not allow it in right now, is the place where I shut off from *you.* When I shut off from hurt, I shut off from life itself. And when I am shut off from life, I am shut off from the one in front of me, who is also life itself.

If I want to love you—really love you—I must find the place where I can love the hurt as well. I must discover the place where hurt is already loved. If I want to have an open heart, if I want to stay radically open to you, I must fully open up to pain in this moment. That's the deal. Otherwise, I become the hurt one—or the unloved one or the helpless one or the one in pain. I am shut off from you, and my heart is closed. From that place, I can only *try* to love you. As the hurt one, I cannot truly love. I can only try to "do love."

Love is not something you do; it's what you are. It is naturally there when hurt is deeply accepted in this moment. In deep acceptance, I realize that I am not the hurt one at all. The image of myself as the hurt one is crucified by the hurt itself. The hurt, deeply allowed, destroys my image of myself as the hurt one. And I relax into the wide-open space in which all hurt can appear and disappear. I am vast enough to allow all hurt into myself. Who I am can never, ever be hurt by you, or by anyone. In this place, you are no longer the one who hurt me, I am no longer your victim, and so we can finally meet. Here, you can never, ever be my enemy. Here, I never need to fear you.

And so, can I simply be here, with any hurt that appears when you tell me your truth?

I must be honest with myself. What may appear in present experience is an urge, in response to the hurt, to lash out at you. Can that urge be allowed too, if it's there? I'm not going to pretend that it's not there. This is about radical honesty with my experience. The hurt is there, and the urge to hurt you is there.

Can I simply be here with the hurt and the urge to escape the hurt? This can be a wonderful place to sit without any expectation.

I begin to notice that both hurt and my urge to escape the hurt are allowed in the space that I am. Both the hurt and my inability to allow the hurt totally are embraced by the deepest acceptance of life. This is radical forgiveness, isn't it?

Can I find this deepest acceptance right here, in the moment, where I feel more of an urge than ever to hurt another human being? Can the end of war be found here, right at the point when the war is about to begin? Can an urge simply be seen as another wave of the ocean, already accepted by the ocean that I am?

This can be a very strange thing indeed—to allow an urge to hurt someone, especially if we are trying to hold onto an image of ourselves as a good person or a kind person or a loving person or even a pure, perfect, nonviolent spiritual being who never feels "negative" things toward anyone!

We have been taught that we shouldn't feel negatively toward anyone. We have been taught that we should feel only kind feelings, think only good thoughts. We fear that if we allow an urge of that kind, we will end up *acting* on it. But this conditioning is false when tested against reality. An urge that is denied, rejected, pushed away will tend to grow and grow. An urge that is denied will become *urgent,* and at some point, it will feel that we have no choice but to act on it. But to deeply allow an urge fully, to allow an urge to be there—not to reject it, not to do anything with it, not to judge it, but just to allow it exactly as it is, without expectation, without even the expectation that the urge will go away—is to *take the urgency out of the urge.* This doesn't mean the urge goes away, but it no longer threatens to take you over, so to speak. It no longer feels dangerous or threatening. It no longer defines you. Often the most violent people are the ones who are the most repressed emotionally. They try hard to keep their feelings and urges *down*—feelings of sadness, of powerlessness, of fear, of failure and impotence—and because of that repression, these feelings and urges end up bursting out in other, destructive ways.

So we come to see that the strangest and strongest urges are allowed in what we are. The most intense waves are already allowed into this ocean. There is no part of experience that the ocean does not love. We will see in the next chapter how this realization can help us to break addictions open and find the freedom within even the strongest cravings.

Remember, acceptance doesn't mean that the pain or the hurt *goes away.* I think that's a huge mistake that people make. They expect that once they discover this deepest acceptance, all the hurt and pain and strange urges will magically disappear. When these things don't disappear, they feel more hurt and confused and more of a failure than ever. The deepest acceptance has failed, which makes them the deepest failure! But the idea that any wave should go away is just the seeker talking. And that's okay too, if it happens. The feeling of being a failure at getting rid of the waves is allowed to arise here too!

There can be hurt. There can be the urge to get rid of hurt, the urge to lash out and hurt back. And there can be the wish that all of this would go away. *All* is allowed here, in this moment. Everything that is happening in this moment is deeply allowed. No wave can hurt you—even if the wave hurts. I never cease to be amazed at the all-encompassing nature of awareness. It is so radically loving, so unconditional in its embrace that there is never a single thought, feeling, sensation, smell, sound that it rejects. It even allows rejection into itself. Love your enemy, indeed.

And so, in the name of true love, I drop all ideas of what love is. I drop all ideas of what relationship is. I drop all ideas of how I should or shouldn't think and feel around you. I realize that, just as when I am not around you, I am the wide-open space in which all thoughts and feelings are deeply allowed to come and go, so too when I am around you, I am that same unconditionally accepting open space. If joy, bliss, excitement, and warm, pleasurable feelings come and go in me in your presence, that's wonderful. I love you in the midst of those feelings. But true love is not just about feeling the good stuff. It's not just about the warm, fluffy, pleasurable, romantic feelings. That's a horribly limited idea of love. Love is vast enough to hold anything. If frustration, confusion, hurt, anger, sadness, pain, boredom, and even despair, disgust, and helplessness come and go in me in your presence, I find that these waves are also deeply allowed in what I am too. They are not a threat to love; they are an expression *of* love, however strange that may sound to the conditioned mind. And so, I can still stay radically open to you. I can keep on relating, even in the midst of the most painful or uncomfortable feelings. Why do we see relationships as some kind of protective bubble in which certain waves in the ocean are not allowed? What are we trying to protect, exactly? A secondhand image of what a relationship should look like? Why do we limit our love in this way? A relationship, just like who we really are, is an ocean, vast enough to allow *any* wave.

Try meeting another in this place of deep acceptance, today and for the rest of your life. Because this may be your last moment together and you may not get another chance. Do you really need a future in order to connect *now?*

One of my favorite things to do is sit with my elderly father. It's a beautiful thing just to sit in a place of profound not-knowing with him, a place where I do not know what to say or do. I sit, without expectation, without trying to fix him, without trying to manipulate his or my experience in any way. I just listen, without trying to make things better in the moment, without playing the role of "the one who knows." As the wide-open space of awareness, I am simply available to him, open to whatever happens when we are together. And as I sit with him, I notice a deep and profound acceptance of any wave of frustration or sadness or discomfort that appears in my ocean of experience. His pain, my pain—there is no difference at all. Sometimes I even forget whether it is he or I who is in pain.

This seems to me to be what true relationship is at its very core; it's meeting—really meeting—in this moment, without hope, without a future, without expectation, without a story. Coming face to face with yourself. I love what the spiritual teacher Nisargadatta Maharaj says: "With the dissolution of the personal 'I,' personal suffering disappears." But crucially, he also adds, "What remains is the great sadness of compassion." Yes, the absence of a separate self is not cold detachment and world rejection, but care and intimacy of the most unimaginable kind. For when you are no longer living in fear of life, why would you want or need to cling to anyone, or block anyone out?

The world is not comprehensible, but it is embraceable . . .
MARTIN BUBER

Addictions

We human beings seem to be able to become addicted to pretty much anything. We become addicted to drugs, to cigarettes, to alcohol, to gambling, to painkillers, to shopping, to the Internet and computer games, to extreme and dangerous sports, to food. We become addicted to relationships, to constantly being around other people, to staying in touch with them via our cell phones twenty-four hours a day, to constantly updating everyone we know about our lives on Facebook and Twitter, to making sure they know that we exist and continue to exist. We become addicted to spirituality—to the nonstop reading of spiritual books, to our spiritual teachers and gurus, to attending endless retreats and satsangs. We become addicted to our careers—to working huge numbers of hours per day doing things we don't necessarily even enjoy. And it isn't always because we need so much money that we work; we work because of abstract concepts like status, prestige, duty, security—things we are supposed to believe in, because everyone else seems to. Have we ever questioned if and why *we* believe in them?

We are addicted to material things, to substances, to belief systems, to other people, but at the root of *all* of these addictions is our main addiction: *our addiction to ourselves.* We are addicted to the story of "me." We are addicted to holding up that image of ourselves and defending it to the death; to constantly working on that image, improving it, comparing and contrasting it with other images; to creating the perfect image, completing that image before we die, and making sure that image is upheld by others even after our deaths. In that sense, we are all addicts, whether we like it or not, whether we have a clinical diagnosis of addiction or not.

Is it possible to go beyond the idea of addiction as a disease, to drop all our preconceived notions and take a look with fresh eyes at what is really going on, on the deepest level? I want to go beyond physical, sociological, and psychological explanations and see what is happening on the very deepest level when someone is drawn time and time again, seemingly without their control and often against their will, to behaviors, people, places, or substances that ultimately are no good for them, that do not *heal* them, in the true sense of the word. What are they really looking for?

Addiction is often understood as the inability to stop doing something. At its most extreme, it's when you feel that you need to do something simply to function, just to go on, just to feel okay, *despite* the side effects and the consequences.

It is probably true to say that nobody *intentionally* sets out to get addicted to anything. A cigarette, a drink, or a drug, at first, can be unpleasant, even disgusting. Many addicts say they absolutely hated their first experience of the drug, but simply wanted to experiment, to flirt with danger, or to fit in or feel included. Some people break through this first experiment and start using the substance (or object, person, or experience) more regularly. And as their system becomes more and more tolerant to the substance, they have to take more and more of it in to give them the desired high. In extreme cases, the need for a drug can become all-consuming and take over their lives, destroying their careers, relationships, and health.

I don't feel that psychiatrists, psychologists, sociologists, or any other researchers have ever really gotten to the bottom of *why* some people become addicted and others don't. There are many theories about addiction, but not much understanding of its root causes. For example, a great many people drink alcohol in this world. However, few are heavy drinkers, and even fewer become addicted. Why do some people become addicted and others not? The literature suggests that there are risk factors associated with addiction—such as childhood abuse or neglect, mental illness, poverty, stress, a lack of education—and it is said that there may be a genetic role. It is said that addiction may be inherited, that some people are simply predisposed to becoming addicted to something and there isn't much they can do about it. Many people view addiction as a disease or a brain disorder, and some even say that it's something you never get rid of, that you have to learn to live with it for the rest of your life. Once an addict, always an addict, some say. For some people, addiction really defines who they are. They hold tightly to their image of themselves as an addict.

I don't want to say that anyone is wrong. I just want you to look deeper than perhaps you've ever looked before.

Now, before we go any further, I want to be clear: I'm not suggesting that, if you see yourself as an addict, you should immediately drop all the things you are doing to cure yourself of your addiction. I simply want to present a different perspective on things—and this perspective is not intended to *replace* what you are already doing. I don't want to encourage anyone to leave any rehab clinic, therapy, recovery group, or twelve-step program. Keep doing what you are doing, if it's working for you. But perhaps by taking a fresh look at what is going on at the very deepest level, you may discover a freedom that your current program is not providing.

We can talk about the risk factors of addiction. We can give psychological and physiological explanations. We can detail the behavior of an addict from the outside or from the inside, so to speak. But what is really happening, on the level of present-moment experience, when I reach out for the next drink? What am I trying to do, on the deepest level? What is the *experience* of addiction? *Who* is the addict, really? Until we ask addicts, "Who are you, beyond all your ideas about yourself?" we are not really getting to the root of the problem, and all our solutions will be built on faulty, secondhand assumptions and dualistic thinking.

People we call addicts are basically no different from the rest of us. In a sense, a seeker is always an addict—addicted to the future, addicted to moving away from this moment, addicted to finding release in any way he or she can. We find release through sex, through drugs, through cigarettes, through ear-bleedingly loud music, through finally getting that new Gucci bag or that exclusive sports car or the latest computer game. And for a short while, it seems like we are relieved of the burden of seeking, the burden of lack. For a few precious moments, as I inhale deeply from my cigarette, I forget all my troubles; the past and future fall away or recede into the background, and all that's left is the warm, soothing smoke moving down my throat and into my lungs. The empty feeling has gone away. There is a kind of fullness that seems attainable only with this cigarette. In a way, the cigarette, the glass of wine, the ear-bleedingly loud music become a lover, a mother, a guru, providing the release I crave. It takes me back to the womb. It releases my burdens. It removes discomfort. It brings me home—temporarily.

Many people find release through sex. At the point of climax, the whole world falls away, and there is total union. I am swimming in an ocean of love, and there is just the total simplicity of life as it is, of this moment—just what's happening right now. Everything else falls into oblivion. No wonder the French call this experience *le petit mort,* "the little death." Everything else seems somehow unimportant; the wave collapses into the ocean, I lose myself in life. I am back in the womb. My struggle is dead. My deepest longing is fulfilled—temporarily.

I get the new car, the new house, the new gold watch, and it feels like my seeking is at an end. It truly feels like the sex, the drugs, the cigarette, the money, the fame, have the *power* to take away my pain, the power to complete me, in a way that nothing and nobody else can. For some seekers, the only way they know how to complete themselves is through an addiction object.

It's almost as if we are trying to *obliterate* ourselves through the drugs, the alcohol, the sex. On some level, just as the wave longs to return to the ocean, we also long to shed the burden of the separate self. We long to lose ourselves and be absorbed into life. Returning home from a long and stressful day at the office, I take a drink, and another, and another, and soon all my problems seem so far away, as if they don't exist and never existed. I don't just forget them—they are literally *gone,* in this moment, in my experience. On some level, the addiction object enables us to satisfy the deepest longing that every human has—to disappear, to be absorbed into life, to die into this moment, to come home, to return to the womb, to be relieved of the heavy burden of the separate self, to dissolve back into the ocean, and to rest, finally rest. As I gulp down another pint of beer, as I inject the trendy drug, as I drive home in my new sports car, everything feels *okay*—for a while.

It would be wonderful if this mechanism actually delivered what it promised—permanent completeness. Alas, it does not, because there is always the comedown. The glow wears off. The discomfort resurfaces. The pain returns. The incompleteness comes back, sometimes more intensely than ever, and then I crave my *next* hit, my *next* release, my *next* experience. The seeker reappears, still incomplete, still unsatisfied—maybe more unsatisfied than ever. The empty, unfulfilled feeling resurfaces; the sense of lack returns. I go back into the story of my unfulfilled life, and then I long to be free from it all again.

If the seeking mechanism delivered on its promises and really *did* remove this sense of lack, there would be no problem at all. There would be no such thing as addictions. I wouldn't need drugs, cigarettes, food, or sex to take away my pain. I wouldn't feel compelled to indulge so frequently or at all. Life would be in total balance. The fact is, the cigarette doesn't provide wholeness. It doesn't take away my problems; it doesn't take away discomfort for long. *But maybe the next one will.* The drug high doesn't last, but maybe next time it will. I win at gambling, and it doesn't satisfy. But maybe if I win again, if I win more, I will be satisfied. We always seek the next release, and the cycle goes on.

You see, we aren't really addicted to cigarettes; we're addicted to the apparent *release,* the absorption into life, the temporary reprieve from lack that the cigarette *seems* to bring. We aren't really addicted to sex; we're addicted to the release it apparently gives, the falling away of the burden of "me." We aren't really addicted to gambling; it's just that gambling takes us out of ourselves for a few precious minutes, hours, days. We aren't really addicted to objects or people; we're addicted to the release they seem to bring.

The seeker is addicted to release. It's the wave seeking the ocean again. What a relief it is, for a moment, to think you've found what you're looking for! What a relief to be the ocean, if only for a few perfect moments! And what hell it is to lose that relief and be dragged back into the world of human problems so quickly!

Alcohol addiction; substance addiction; gambling addiction; sexual addiction; addictions to people, to gurus, to money, to fame—it seems as though there are many different kinds of addiction. In fact, there is only one addiction: the seeker's addiction to release. And when you understand this, what the addiction object actually is becomes less important. Often, in trying to cure ourselves of addictions, we focus way too much on the details of the addiction object and on the story of our addiction, and not on the root mechanism that is fueling the need for the object. I may be healed from my cigarette addiction, but if I don't face the underlying lack, the addiction will pop up in some other area of my life. I have known people who quit smoking after twenty years and then immediately started overeating. People who are addicted to relationships break up from their current relationship and immediately get into drugs. People who have an addiction to shopping suddenly drop that addiction and become addicted to a spiritual guru. Any addiction cure or remedy or therapy that focuses on the addiction object rather than the seeking in the addict will not truly resolve addiction. It may help, but it won't heal, in the true sense of the word.

Whether it's a cigarette, a bottle of beer, or the thrill of the promise of winning a million on roulette, every addiction object serves the same purpose: it seems to take away the discomfort of this moment as it is. It promises release, and it seems to deliver that release for a while. But it doesn't really provide what we truly long for.

Often addicts talk about "getting their fix." What are they trying to fix? Deep down, although they probably don't know it, they are trying to fix a primal sense of separation, trying to fix incompleteness. As we have seen time and time again in this book, nothing and nobody can fix separation and incompleteness; no external object or person can do this. The only fix for incompleteness is a radical and total embrace of that very incompleteness—the embrace that you are in your essence. That's what we really long for, deep down—*intimacy with ourselves.*

Of course, we don't pick up a cigarette or a painkiller or a bottle of beer because we think, "I'm feeling incomplete, and this will complete me." No, we simply feel *an urge, a craving.* We feel strangely *drawn* to our object of addiction, almost against our will. "If I had the choice," I say to myself, "I wouldn't be doing this." But it feels like I have no choice. The cigarette seems to have a strange *power* over me. Gambling, sex, money—they seem to have a strange *power* over me, a mysterious power that drags me in, no matter how much I protest. The chocolate—it just sits there in the cupboard, calling to me. *Eat me. Eat me. I will make you feel better.* The beer sits there, like the devil tempting me, promising release. *Go on. Just a little sip . . .*

It's not an intellectual thing; you don't consciously realize you're seeking. You just *find yourself* picking up a cigarette. You find yourself downing another vodka. You find yourself stuffing your face with chocolate. And it feels like you can't do anything about it. It *feels* like you are somehow being controlled by the object of addiction and it's all out of your hands. Yes, that's how it *feels*—like we are victims of addiction. That something called "addiction" is happening to someone called "me."

This power that we seem to feel emanating from the object of addiction is the same power I have been talking about throughout this book. When we believe that an object, substance, or person is able to complete us in some way, we project a kind of mysterious power onto it. Whether it's food, a spiritual guru, a lover, a celebrity, a political or religious leader, a bottle of whisky, or a cigarette, it can really feel like it has power over you, like it has some kind of aura, a kind of compelling, magnetic energy emanating from it. It appears to radiate power.

But this isn't real power. Nothing and no one has that kind of power—the power to complete you. No wave possesses any more power than any other wave; every wave is equally ocean. Power is never external, in that sense. What you experience as power "out there" in the world is simply *your own power, projected.* It is life power projected outward and focused on another object or person. The power isn't really in the object or person, although that's what it *seems* like, that's what it *feels* like, that's what it tastes and smells like. Power doesn't belong to anyone or anything, for life itself is the only power.

This idea—that completion resides "out there," in time and space, in the world, that some people or objects have it and others don't—is the projection that keeps the seeking going. *The seeker must always hold the end of seeking outside of him- or herself, in order to stay alive. The seeker must project sources of invisible power out there, in the visible world, and then seek that power.* Since the dawn of humanity, we have been projecting power "out there"—onto the sun, onto the stars, onto animals, onto nature, onto inanimate objects, onto other people. Humans have always had gods. Even atheists are deeply religious in this sense.

The seeker of release projects the power of release onto an object, in the same way that the seeker of enlightenment projects that very enlightenment onto a person, and the seeker of love focuses their longing onto a person, giving that object the apparent power to complete them. The upshot is that it feels like you really *need* the object. It feels like you *need* your fix. It feels like you need sex, you need chocolate, you need a drink, you need a cigarette, you need to go to another satsang or retreat, you need to hang around your guru or love object, in order to be whole again.

You could say that *need* is how the seeking mechanism manifests itself in our experience. We don't experience the seeking mechanism directly; we experience need, longing, desire, craving, powerlessness in the face of life. We will never truly understand desire until we understand the seeking mechanism behind it. It's an astonishingly creative mechanism that seems to keep you from an awareness of who you really are. It's when we don't see this mechanism for what it is, when we get caught up in seeking, rather than *seeing* the seeking and recognizing ourselves as the wide-open space of awareness in which seeking happens, that we suffer, and we reach out to escape our suffering.

Now, stuffing your face with chocolate all the time wouldn't be a problem if, after a while, it didn't make you obese and prone to heart attacks and strokes. There is nothing wrong with eating chocolate, *in itself.* That's part of life too. It's when the chocolate is being used to provide release—that's when the problem begins. It's the seeking *through* chocolate that's the problem. Chocolate + seeking = addiction.

In the same way, alcohol, in itself, is not wrong or evil or bad, but part of life. Alcohol is a neutral substance that we don't *need* to use in the way we do. It's when we use alcohol to distract ourselves from what's really going on, to take away discomfort, to provide completeness, to escape from this moment as it is—that's when the trouble begins. Alcohol + seeking = addiction.

In the same way, money, in itself, is not evil. It's the use of money—the way we hoard it for ourselves, the way we hurt and kill to get others' money, the competition and jealousy it can lead to when our feelings of inadequacy and power-lessness are not deeply accepted—that we might call "evil." Money itself has no evil power residing in it. Nothing does.

You get the picture. Substances and activities—sex, drink-ing, eating chocolate, waging bets at the casino or on the stock market—in themselves, are not problems. These can all be fun, enjoyable, innocent parts of life. It's when the seeker starts to *use* these activities to get something that the problems start.

When you're seeking something through a cigarette, you're not really smoking a cigarette anymore. You barely even notice the actual moment-by-moment experience of smoking the cigarette. You're not really present with the experience, because you're anticipating the high too much. You're not really smoking the cigarette—you're trying to smoke wholeness. *You're not really smoking the cigarette—you're using it to get somewhere.* You've stopped seeing—really seeing—what's in front of you. You're seeking a future moment. This moment has become a means to an end. You're trying to move from here to there, using the poor little cigarette.

Making the cigarette into the enemy isn't going to help. That's what a lot of self-help books and courses about addiction seem to imply—that the cigarette, the alcohol, the drugs are some kind of enemy, that they are evil, that we should wage war against them, perhaps for the rest of our lives.

I want to present another way of looking at addictions. The cigarette is not the enemy. When you see—really see— this seeking mechanism at work, in all its intricacies and subtleties, you see how the cigarette is innocent. It has no power over you and never did. You were using it to try to reach wholeness. You became a user, in the true sense of the word. The cigarette was always innocent, always neutral, and in your pursuit of release, you used it and then forgot why you were using it (if you ever knew in the first place). And then you turned around and blamed it for casting a spell over you. It was really the other way around—you cast a spell over it. In your innocence, in your search for wholeness, you projected completion power onto it. You made it symbolize the end of seeking. You turned it into your guru, giving it a power it never had and never could have.

This is not about blaming anyone—the cigarette *or* the one who smokes it. It's not that the cigarette is innocent, and you are guilty. You are both innocent. When you are caught up in seeking, you have no choice but to reach out to anything you perceive as giving release. In your innocence, you reach out to the cigarette. When you feel like you need something, it also feels like you have *no choice* but to go get what you need. You are innocent in your seeking. So I'm not blaming anyone. The blame-and-shame game is not necessary here. This is simply about *seeing* what's going on in your own experience, and not judging yourself for it.

URGES, CRAVINGS, NEEDS, AND WANTS

What does an urge feel like? What does a craving feel like? What does it feel like when you *need* something?

It's very hard to describe or define exactly what a craving or an urge is. Again, we talk about urges, cravings, or needs as if we know exactly what we are talking about. But, as we have been doing throughout this book, let's go beyond the story, the story of the urge, and come back to the actual moment-by-moment experience of it. Beyond the story, what is actually happening?

I'm sitting in my favorite chair, reading a book. Nothing is missing. There is simply life happening—sounds, smells, thoughts, feelings, all coming and going. I'm enjoying the simplicity of this moment.

Suddenly, I find myself craving—craving a cigarette. What just happened? Let's come back to the actual experience and walk through it in slow motion.

First there was an uncomfortable feeling. Something suddenly felt unsatisfied and incomplete, and it wanted to be complete again. It wanted to reach out—for a cigarette, the thing it thought would take away the incompleteness. And there was an urge to smoke—in other words, an urge to find completeness through smoking. Smoking would take away the discomfort.

There's something *urgent* about an urge, isn't there? An urge is never a relaxed, laid-back, easy experience. Something feels tight and contracted. It feels like something needs to be satisfied *urgently*. Suddenly, there is an urgency to life. It feels like you need a cigarette right now—not tomorrow, not a little bit later, but *now*.

A few moments ago, life seemed complete. I was comfortable in the chair, reading my book. Nothing was missing. Now, suddenly, it feels like there is something *missing* from present experience. A hole has opened up in present experience. It feels like there is the lack of something. What is lacking? What will fill the hole? What will end the lack? Is it really possible for nothing to be missing and then, in the blink of an eye, for something to be missing?

All urges—in fact, all seeking—always begin with a general sense of lack, and then this general lack becomes the lack of something specific.

What is missing? Ah, I know. A *cigarette* is missing from present experience. The hole is a cigarette-shaped hole. If I were smoking right now, the present experience would be complete. The cigarette would take away the hole.

The original meaning of the word *want* was "lack." It is only for the past few hundred years that *want* has been synonymous with *desire*. And so when I say, "I want a cigarette right now," what I really mean is, "I feel as though I lack a cigarette right now. A cigarette is missing." A moment ago, a cigarette wasn't missing. Then suddenly, it is missing.

Suddenly, I lack a cigarette; suddenly, I want a cigarette— same thing.

But a cigarette is not really missing from present experience. Present experience is always complete in itself. Nothing can ever be missing from present experience, just as the ocean is never missing, no matter which waves are appearing. It's only thought that would say, "Something is missing." But even the thought that something is missing is simply appearing in this open space. *The thought and feeling that something's missing* are not missing here! They are fully present. Nothing, literally nothing, is missing here.

The beginning of great freedom is to realize that *nothing is ever missing from present experience*. There is only ever the *story* that something is missing, the feeling that something is missing. And all stories and their associated feelings appear in the wide-open space that you are, which is always complete in itself. Nothing is missing from the open space that you are, because the open space that you are holds *everything* as it comes and goes. Even the strongest feeling of lack appears and disappears in what you are. Even lack is part of the completeness of this moment. Here, where you are, even lack is complete.

Here's a wonderful analogy: Imagine you're watching a movie scene in which some characters are sitting around a dinner table, talking about another character, whom they say is missing from the dinner table. But from your perspective, as the viewer, is the character really missing? Is the character missing from the scene? No, the scene is complete in itself. Those characters sitting around a dinner table and talking about someone who's missing constitute a complete scene in the movie. Nothing is *ever* missing from a scene in a movie. You never watch a scene in a movie and say to yourself, "Hmm, that's strange. There's something missing from this scene." Even if the scene is *about* someone who is missing, you know that in truth there is nothing and nobody missing. No character can ever be missing from a movie. A scene in a movie is always complete. In the same way, when a loved one dies, and you miss them, are they truly missing? Nothing and nobody is missing from the ocean of life.

So it's a lie, a great big lie, to say that a cigarette is *missing*. Your *lack* of a cigarette is a lie. Your *want* of a cigarette is a lie.

I want to make it clear that, ultimately, there's nothing wrong with having wants in life. Here we risk the danger of falling into another spiritual trap. Over the years, I've met many people who were desperately trying to get rid of all their wants, because they thought that was the way to enlightenment. They truly believed that an enlightened person doesn't have any wants.

First, their want to get rid of all wants is the biggest want of all.

Second, a life without any wants would be a very dull life indeed. I doubt it's possible to be a living, breathing human being and not experience wants. I want to visit an art gallery. I want a cup of tea. I want to visit my beloved parents. You've tripped, and I want to help you off the ground. I want to have a child. I want you to read my book. I want to be honest with you about how I feel. I want to break free from this prisoner-of-war camp. These are all perfect expressions of life in themselves, and to deny wants, or to try to pretend that you don't have them, can be very unhealthy indeed. Trying to get rid of all wants is just part of the seeking game.

I think it would help to distinguish between authentic, healthy wants, such as, "I want to go to the park today," and wants that are based on a sense of lack—you could call them *seeking wants*—such as, "I want a cigarette because without it I'm incomplete." I think this is a hugely important distinction to make.

It does seem that a lot of spiritual teachings talk about wants as negative things. "Wants are ego. Wants are all selfish. Wants are delusion. Wants are dualistic. Wants always lead to suffering, and if we want to end suffering, we should rid ourselves of all wants, all desire, all attachment. We should aim to live in a state of not wanting anything. We should stop wanting money. We should stop wanting possessions. We should give away everything we have and live on the streets. Then we'll be free. We should stop wanting sex. We should give up all desire for sex and live a life of chastity. Then we will be pure and closer to God. We should stop wanting pleasure, because pleasure is bad and unspiritual, and if we shut ourselves off from all sources of happiness in life, then we will be enlightened." That's what some spiritual teachings seem to be saying.

But the flip side of all of this giving up of wants is that we end up leading dull, lifeless, disconnected lives—and we end up always *at war* with our wants. Secretly we don't really get rid of our wants, so we just repress them. We repress our desire for sex, for example, by pretending to ourselves and to others that we're free from it, and yet secretly our desire for sex goes on. And the more we try to bury it, the more it threatens to burst out—until finally it does. And we can easily see the consequences of that. Just look at the many scandals concerning supposedly celibate religious leaders in the last century. Anything we try to repress must come out eventually in some distorted form. The life force simply wants to express itself; it won't be restrained.

Recently, a woman was telling me about her less-than-joyful twenty-year marriage to her husband. In the past few years, she had become a spiritual seeker and had spent many hours practicing a method that aimed to rid her of all her desires in her marriage—because desires, she had come to learn, were unreasonable demands to place on another human being. Once she stopped wanting anything from her husband, she'd be free. She called this method "getting rid of her ego."

Well, she'd managed to rid herself of all her wants. And in one sense, this was a wonderful thing. Many, many of her wants had been unreasonable demands on her husband and had been an expression of her seeking; they had been ways of trying to make her husband into something he just couldn't be for her. Trying to fix him had brought her much suffering. So it was a relief to her to be free from those unreasonable, seeking-based wants.

But she had gone too far and erased *all* wants. And her relationship with her husband was no better. She had erased everything; in fact, there was now barely any relationship left between them. The relationship had died.

I asked her, "Tell me, what do you want from a relationship?"

She hesitated and replied, "Oh, I thought I wasn't supposed to want anything."

I asked her again. She thought for a long time, but couldn't come up with anything.

"Okay, let me help you out," I said. "What about something simple, like having someone you could talk to?"

"Oh yes, I'd like that, of course. That would be wonderful," she replied.

I found this answer very moving. There was a genuine want there, an authentic want that wasn't coming from seeking, from a sense of lack. It was coming from her heart. It was a beautiful, passionate expression of life in itself. It was an authentic, genuine want that had been buried in her quest to be free from all wants. This little want simply hadn't had the chance to breathe. In destroying all wants, she'd destroyed the genuine, authentic wants. She'd thrown the babies out with the bathwater.

Not all wants are expressions of lack. When we express a genuine, healthy want, we are saying something like this: "I want this. I would like to experience this. But whether or not I get what I want, I'm still absolutely okay. Not getting what I want isn't going to detract one iota from this present okayness."

There's a difference between wanting a cigarette and wanting a cigarette *to complete you,* which a cigarette cannot do. Wanting a cigarette is not a problem, until you want a cigarette *in order to take away discomfort.* Then you have a want that stems from seeking, a want that is an expression of lack, and that is a want that will lead directly to suffering and more lack. You are saying, "I want this, and if I don't get it, I won't be okay. Only getting what I want can make things okay." That's a want based on the illusion of lack, the illusion that there is something missing, and the illusion that only a cigarette can fill the void. Now we're no longer seeing reality as it is; we've moved into seeking. We move into a dream and, therefore, suffering.

MEETING AN URGE

You're probably thinking, "I can understand intellectually that the cigarette won't make me complete, but it still feels as though I need a cigarette!" An urge feels *physical.* A want feels *physical.* Before you know it, it really does feel like your body *needs* a fix. As noted before, the body cannot tell the difference between a real and imagined threat; neither can it tell the difference between a real lack and imagined lack.

The reality is that the body never needs a cigarette. *You* do. The seeker does. The body is not trying to complete itself. *You* are. I think one of the big lies that we tell is "My body needs the cigarette" or "I can't live without the cigarette" or "I'll die without my cigarette." Well yes, it can *feel* that way. But just because you feel that way doesn't mean the need is real.

What we really mean by "I need a cigarette" is "I am unwilling to experience the discomfort of not having the cigarette." And there it is: I don't want to experience the *discomfort*—the incompleteness, the pain, the hurt, the not-okayness—of not getting what I want. I don't want those waves to come. I feel like I'll drown in them. I feel like I'll be overwhelmed by them. I won't be able to handle them. I feel like I'll die without my addiction object, without my escape route, without anything to subdue the pain of existence.

When the hope of completion is stripped away from the seeker, what's left? When time is stripped away, when all hope of getting what you want and being complete disappears, what are you left with?

You're left with what is. You're left with your discomfort, your incompleteness, everything you were running away from, without any hope of escaping it. You're left facing life as it is—facing those rejected waves, the thoughts and feelings you've been running away from, perhaps all your life. You're left facing your pain, your sadness, your guilt, your regret, your loneliness, your worst fears. You're left here, now, in this moment, facing what is.

To a separate person, being faced with all of these things is a major problem. But in the open space that you are, there is no problem—every wave can simply be there. The extreme discomfort. A sense of lack. An urge to smoke. A craving, a want. The sense that something needs to complete itself. Pain. Agitation. Perhaps heart palpitations. Sweating. All sorts of images—of how awful your life is, of you smoking the cigarette in bliss, of yourself deeply inhaling the cool smoke, of all the relaxation it will bring, of the release of it. The release is so close, you can almost touch it.

There's a desperate urge to reach out and light up. In one moment, all this discomfort could be wiped out. In one moment, hell could turn to heaven. The anticipation feels unbearable. You desperately want a cigarette. The cigarette will take all of this discomfort away. Just one tiny, little cigarette. Just a few moments away. Go on. Just one little cigarette. Oh, it's *so* tempting.

As we have seen, you don't really want a cigarette. What you really want is for the present moment to be deeply okay again. *What you really want is to no longer be in want. What you really want is to no longer be in lack.* What you really want is for all of this discomfort to be *deeply accepted.* You want to be deeply okay where you are; you want to be at home here and now, and you think having a cigarette is the only way to get there.

"I want a cigarette"—that is a lie. It's a lie based on mis-identification, a lie based on huge assumptions about who you really are, a lie that comes from not seeing the wholeness of your present experience.

Now, I'm not telling you to *pretend* that you don't want a cigarette. Pretending never works—it only leads to more pretending. I'm not telling you to pretend that you don't have urges or cravings. You're a human being, not a robot. I'm asking you to honor the want, but also trying to get you to dive into the heart of the want—to drop all your assumptions and see with fresh eyes what it really is, beyond what you've been told it is, what you assume it is, what you believe it is.

We've pushed right through the experience of craving to discover the simple seeking mechanism at the core of it. *The longing is not for a cigarette (or a drink or sex or the next high), but for the deepest acceptance.* We don't long for a cigarette; we long for the intimacy of present-moment awareness—the open space in which every wave of experience is accepted. We don't really crave a cigarette; we long for our craving of a cigarette to be deeply okay. We long to love our craving as it is, however crazy that sounds at first.

When a craving is simply allowed to be there, with all the discomfort that entails, and when the urge to escape the discomfort is simply allowed to be there—when every thought, every sensation, every feeling is simply allowed to be there, and when this present experience is seen to be deeply accepted right now—I no longer *need* the cigarette to complete me. *This is where the cycle of need can be broken—right at the very heart of that need.* This is freedom *in* need—freedom *in* craving, not freedom *from* craving. This is about discovering the freedom in which the craving and the urge to satisfy that craving both appear and are allowed to appear, just as all waves in the ocean are already allowed by the ocean.

It's not about fighting the craving or ignoring the craving. It's about deeply allowing the craving to be there, along with any urge, even a desperate urge, to satisfy the craving. An urge and an urge to satisfy that urge are the best of friends. If you are to sit with an urge, you must also welcome in its best friend, the urge to escape that urge, and discover the place where both are deeply allowed in what you are.

Allowing a craving—just sitting with it, watching all the images that float by, feeling all the sensations as they come and go, really allowing yourself to deeply feel the urge to have a cigarette, allowing the discomfort, allowing even the strongest urge, the urge that's so strong you feel as though you're *about* to act on it, to be there—can be a very strange experience. Remember, there's no urge too strong for this deepest acceptance to "handle." You feel as though you're about to die without a cigarette, and still, even within that feeling, the deepest acceptance is still there. The deepest acceptance can hold that feeling too. *It's unbearable. I can't go on.* That one too. *This is too uncomfortable. I can't stand it.* That one too. *I'm about to die. I can't take it anymore.* That one too. *I'm dying!* You're still alive. *I can't handle it!* You're handling it. *I can't bear it!* You're bearing it.

What I've discovered is this: even without the cigarette, even with all of these feelings that are appearing in the absence of a cigarette, even in the experience of *not getting what I think I want,* I am deeply okay. Even without the cigarette, I am complete in this present experience. In the midst of the most intense craving, this deepest acceptance is still absolutely present. It doesn't mean the craving goes away, but it means my relationship with the craving transmutes. It's no longer a separate wave to be rejected—it's an expression of the ocean to be embraced.

And out of this completeness, I am still free to have a cigarette or not. This is crucial. I am free to smoke, but *I no longer need to do so* to provide completeness. Having a cigarette and not having a cigarette become strangely *equal* in essence. In this deepest acceptance, I end up getting what the cigarette could never give me—freedom to have a cigarette *or not.* I am no longer bound. I am no longer controlled. I am released from the clutches of my guru. The spell is broken. I leave the cigarette cult. I am no longer powerless. I am no longer a victim.

To put it more simply, when a want—for a cigarette, for a drink, for sex, for a trip to the casino, for a bar of chocolate—is deeply allowed, allowed to be as it is, the want is no longer a want in the true sense of the word. In other words, when a want is deeply allowed, it is no longer an expression of lack; it is no longer an expression *of* incompleteness and no longer a search *for* completeness. Now it is simply a bunch of sensations appearing and disappearing in what you are— sensations that are deeply allowed to appear and disappear in what you are, even if they are uncomfortable right now. Wants come and go, and what you are remains. The end of addiction is in a deep and total embrace of wanting, however paradoxical that may sound at first.

Again, notice that I'm not asking you to fight the want, and I'm not telling you to ignore or reject the want or to practice abstinence. Deep acceptance isn't about any kind of self-denial. I'm not saying, "Don't give yourself what you want, and *try* to be happy with not getting it." I'm not asking you to *tolerate* anything.

I can already hear criticisms of this message: "Jeff Foster is telling us to stop having what we want. He says we should be okay with not getting what we want, that we should deny ourselves pleasure! It all sounds so defeatist, so life-denying, so depressing!"

Actually, I'm not saying that *you should be okay* with not getting what you want. I'm inviting you to drop all your previous conclusions and to look again—to see if you can *find* the okayness, in the deepest sense, in the experience of not getting what you want. See if that is a possibility in your world. Finding the place of deepest acceptance is not about tolerating or putting up with not getting what you want; it's about finding the place where even intolerance and frustration are accepted.

And I'm asking you to question the very idea that getting what you want is actually what you really want and, underneath that, to question the idea that you are a separate person who wants something. That's very different from *pretending to be okay* with not getting what you want. It is very different from denying yourself pleasure, which is how the mind may interpret this idea. I'm asking you to see if you can find the okayness in not getting what you thought you wanted, but never really wanted.

It can be a very strange thing to deeply allow a want. Most of the time we're either trying to ignore a want (which only makes the want grow) or we're indulging the want. Deeply accepting the want is the middle way. Between rejecting and indulging lies *seeing*—and allowing, and finding freedom in even the most uncomfortable places.

So your new spiritual practice is this: Sit with discomfort, and with its best friend, the urge to escape that discomfort. Sit without doing anything about them. Sit without expecting them to change. Sit without trying to fix yourself. Sit without hope of any particular outcome. And notice that every thought, every sensation, every feeling—including any expectation, frustration, lack of acceptance, or attempt to change this moment—has already been allowed into this moment. Find the okayness in the midst of the not-okayness. Find the place where this moment is okay, even if it feels uncomfortable and not okay. That place is freedom. That place is what you are. And if that place cannot be found right now, and any feelings of failure arise, deeply allow those too. Simply notice whatever is here, and notice that whatever is here has already been allowed in. This noticing is the very essence of meditation.

And, yes, it can become *very* uncomfortable in this place of no escape. I know of one heroin addict who was quitting the drug cold turkey. His girlfriend told me that his withdrawal symptoms were horrific—terrible cramps all over his body, profuse sweating and shaking, hallucinations. Many times he thought he was going to die. He would call his girlfriend and scream into the phone, "I can't take it anymore! I'm going to die!" Interestingly, it was never *this* round of muscle cramps that was going to kill him—it was the *next* round. It was always *going to* kill him—it hadn't killed him *yet*. The seeker always lives in memories of how bad things were and in anticipation of how bad things might become. The seeker always lives in time.

Eventually his girlfriend, mainly out of the fear that he really wasn't going to make it (even though she'd seen him go through these kind of withdrawal symptoms before and survive them) agreed to drive him across town to his drug dealer to get his fix. In the car on the way there, his condition suddenly improved. As soon as he knew he was going to get his fix, he relaxed. He was still jittery and anxious and in some pain, but he was no longer panicking and threatening that he was about to die. The drug had come to represent freedom from death, and when he knew the drug was available to him, his system relaxed.

Faced with the impossibility of getting what you want, faced with the failure of your search, you can experience total powerlessness, total helplessness, total fear, total lack of control. It really does feel that you are about to die. You come up against everything you wanted to escape, against your own powerlessness in the face of life. Facing these things is very much like facing death. Add to this physical pain of the body readjusting itself, and you have a seemingly unbearable situation that can only be solved—or so it seems—by another hit.

The seeking mechanism can be brutal and withdrawal horribly uncomfortable—let's not pretend otherwise. But can you see that contained within even the most extreme discomfort is an invitation to wholeness? Can you see that even when the waves are uncomfortable, the ocean is still present? It's an invitation that never disappears, no matter what is happening.

The body may be shaking uncontrollably. There may be terrible pain. There may even be the feeling that "I'm about to die" or "I can't take this anymore." But what I am is the open space in which all of these sensations and feelings are unfolding. The pain, the fear, the frustration, even the feelings of helplessness and blind panic—these waves are not really a problem to who I am. They are part of life's constant invitation; they are deeply allowed in what I am. They are there to be noticed, to be seen as part of life—they are not a threat to life. They are not evil, not enemies, not impurities to be destroyed. They are only beloved parts of myself. And I am the calm at the center of this storm. The body does its thing, and what I am never needs to escape what's happening, even if there is the urge to escape what's happening. Here, where I am, it's always okay, in a way I will never be able to explain.

Ending addictions has nothing to do with getting rid of cravings. It's about seeing cravings for what they are and deeply allowing them to be there. Yes, in the end, this freedom is even there in *not getting what you want.* This realization challenges all conventional wisdom, goes against much of our conditioning, and isn't taught in any positive-thinking or self-help books. In a society where so much emphasis is placed on getting what you want, and where getting what you want is said to lead to happiness, it sounds almost crazy to suggest that you could be free and happy in not getting what you want. Perhaps in a mad, mad world, you have to be mad to be sane!

When you discover who you really are, you're free whether you get what you want or not. Either way, you are complete— and no amount of cigarettes, alcohol, sex, food, or money can give you that, just as the absence of these cannot take it away.

WHAT YOU ARE IS NOT AN ADDICT

Is an addict who you really are? Does your addiction define you? Is it really true that, at a base level, there is something wrong with you? Any therapy or recovery program that doesn't first get to the bottom of these questions is surely only going to perpetuate illusions. I'm not saying you should give up everything you're doing already to find freedom from your addiction. But armed with this deeper understanding of who you really are, I'm sure any recovery plan will only be more effective.

And who knows? Maybe at some point you won't need any more recovery plans. You will find yourself having the urge to reach for your next fix, and you will find a deep okayness *within* that very urge, within any discomfort that appears. You will find freedom in everything you were running away from, and in that place of total acceptance, you will discover that what you are is not an addict. You will discover that there is nothing wrong with you. What you are has never wanted or needed to use anything to escape this moment. What you are deeply allows this moment to be as it is.

A man who once defined himself as an alcoholic said to me, "I never stopped drinking. I never stopped being an addict. I just never took the *next* drink."

In this moment of not drinking, are you a drinker? In this moment of not smoking, are you a smoker? In this moment of not reaching out to your addiction object, are you addicted? In this moment, are you an addict?

Perhaps one day—and that day could be today—you will find a cigarette or a drink or a piece of chocolate in front of you, and finally you will know, on the deepest level, that it won't give you anything that isn't already right here. It won't make this experience any more complete than it already is. You can honor the appearance of any urge. You can honor the urge to act on the urge. You can honor any discomfort at not getting what you want. And you can simply let it all be here, as it is, without having to change it in any way.

If you're going to channel your seeking energies, channel them right back here, to when you actually are, and embrace everything that is happening right now. Let go of your search for a future moment when you will be free from addiction, and discover what is really here, right now. And perhaps soon this will become the overriding urge— to accept this moment totally. Perhaps you will become addicted to the deepest acceptance of this moment. That's an addiction you'll never need to recover from, an addiction with no known side effects. And then, even in the midst of pain and discomfort and mysterious urges that you cannot control or even name, perhaps you will come to remember what you have always known, deep down, and what Julian of Norwich said so well: "All shall be well, and all shall be well, and all manner of things shall be well."

It is truth that liberates, not your effort to be free.
KRISHNAMURTI

The Search for Spiritual Enlightenment

Our deepest fear is not the fear of death; it is the fear of life. It is the fear of living—really living—of truly being alive and awake in the here and now, of being unprotected in the face of the raw and wild energy that is life itself. As we have seen, life includes everything—not just the good stuff or the positive stuff or the happy stuff—just as the ocean includes every possible wave, and so to truly be alive and awake, we must open ourselves up to all of it. *All of it.* Yes, life is joy and bliss and happiness, but it is also pain and sadness, fear, anger, confusion, and helplessness. Waking up means admitting that you cannot protect yourself from any of the waves in the ocean of life, that who you really are is so vast and unconditional and free that it cannot help but allow everything in. Opening yourself up to life is equal to opening yourself up to death—the death of who you thought you were, the death of who you believed yourself to be, the death of your own imagination of yourself. Life and death are truly equal, and the mind will never, ever understand this.

People often think that spiritual enlightenment has something to do with getting rid of all the waves of experience they are afraid of. Our misconception about enlightenment is that it is a special state or experience, a place where there is no fear, no pain, no sadness, no anger, nothing negative. In other words, enlightenment is a perfectly calm and controlled ocean, where all the bad waves have died. It is light without darkness, oneness without diversity.

But that view is simply an expression of the longing of the seeker. The seeker wants to numb him- or herself to life. The seeker wants be protected from death, to be in total control of the waves in present experience. Enlightenment, for many people, is the vision of a perfect ocean—an ocean free from all negative waves, all evil waves, all dangerous waves. It is the blissed-out guru, living in a state of perfect happiness, who never feels pain, sadness, boredom, frustration, fear, or any kind of weakness whatsoever. It is freedom from the relative world of pain and suffering. It is an escape from the world of duality. It is the ultimate protection.

We see now that this kind of enlightenment *is not possible*. It is a lie, based on dualistic ideas about who and what we are. It is a dream of the seeker and nothing more. Unfortunately—or perhaps fortunately, in the grand scheme of things—there are many spiritual teachings that cater to that dream. The dream *sells* because it's what the seeker wants more than anything—*comfort, certainty, and security.*

For the whole of human history, out of our basic fear of death (which was secretly our fear of life), we went to war with what we perceived as darkness and pursued what we saw as light. Not recognizing who we really were, we attacked or repressed anything that we saw as threats to that light. We called those aspects of life dangerous, evil, sinful, unholy, wicked—taboos, in the original meaning of the word. Spirituality became a war with darkness, rather than the rediscovery of present light.

Experiencing ourselves as separate individuals, tearing reality into two, we believed that if we could get rid of these dark aspects of our experience, if we could defeat the devil, if we could overcome sin, if we could rid the world of evil, if we could destroy impurity, then we would live long and prosper. In our pursuit of heaven, we created and then went to war with our idea of hell. In our pursuit of nirvana, we rejected samsara. In our pursuit of mental health, we waged war on what we called mental illness. In our pursuit of God, we waged war with sin.

Sin, disease, evil, madness, impurity, anything unholy, anything that didn't fit in with our seeking plans became our taboos, and we felt justified in repressing, fighting, or even destroying them. We created scapegoats, and great violence followed. We believed we were on the side of life and that for our troubles we would be rewarded with more life; we would be protected from death, and all would be well. It made perfect sense—in a way.

Escape the dark and reach the light. Escape the evil and reach the good, the pure, the holy. Escape the personal and reach the impersonal. Escape duality and reach nonduality. That's what we believed, in our innocence.

But when you strip away all religious connotations, words such as *darkness* and *evil* are no longer strange, mystical forces to be feared and fought against, but simply pointers to those waves of experience—those thoughts, sensations, feelings— that are currently being rejected, currently not being seen as expressions of wholeness.

The "evil" or "dark" waves are simply the ones that we mistakenly see as threats *to* wholeness, threats to life. They are the rejected waves. They are the unloved waves. They are the waves we turn our backs on. They are the waves we fear. They are the orphan waves that simply long to come home and are not being allowed in. They are the waves that threaten our precious images of ourselves. Fear, anger, sadness, pain, sexual urges, strange thoughts—these are not inherently dark or evil. They are just not being allowed into the light, and so they *appear* to be something they are not. They appear to be dark and evil and to oppose the light, but in truth, no wave can ever oppose the ocean, for every wave is the ocean. A so-called dark wave doesn't oppose the light; it is already the light, but is not being recognized as such. What we call evil is simply rejected and unloved light. What we call evil is only what we fear.

Many spiritual teachings and practices throughout the ages have been presented to us as ultimate solutions to the problem of being human. We have been taught how to transcend the negative and attract the positive, how to leave the body, how to delete painful emotions, how to escape feelings, how to stop thoughts, how to destroy imperfection and impurity, and how to detach ourselves from life. But why this never-ending battle against thoughts and feelings? Why this war with the present moment? Why do we fear a total embrace of our humanness, the embrace that we actually are in our essence? Why do we fear *ourselves* so much? Why this constant rejection of life itself? Perhaps we fear that if we embrace our humanness fully in the here and now, we will actually be avoiding or missing out on some more sublime existence in the future. We have been led to believe that humanity is in some kind of fallen state, and a full embrace of this fallen, earth-bound, mortal, "illusory" human experience would be a mistake, a cop-out, a giving up, a settling for less than we deserve, a rejection of our cosmic inheritance. We have been taught that beyond the human experience, beyond the shadows in the cave, there is a more perfect world, some immortal, heavenly, and enlightened realm waiting for us.

Perhaps those beliefs are just the dreams and nightmares of the seeker, and the wholeness we seek is already here, actually hidden in our humanness, hidden in everything we are trying to escape. Perhaps being human was never the problem. Perhaps life was never the problem. Perhaps we do not need solutions to the nonexistent problem of being alive here and now. Perhaps we do not need promises of a better world, an afterlife, a heaven, a transcendent spiritual realm, and never did. Perhaps we are deeply okay as we are, already perfect in our imperfection, already fully embraced by the very life we are trying to avoid.

So then, what is enlightenment, if it is not about escaping our humanness, escaping something called negativity or evil or darkness and moving toward something else called light? What is spiritual awakening, if it's not about getting rid of all the stuff we dislike in ourselves? What is ultimate truth, if it is no longer a denial of our humanity? What is the impersonal, if it is no longer at war with the personal? What is the absolute, if it finally embraces the relative? What happens when all waves are *loved*, when there's nobody here separate from life itself? What happens when our fear of death, which is our fear of life, comes to an end?

A man came up to me on the first day of one of my retreats in Holland. He told me that the previous year, after experiencing deep pain and sadness in his life, he had gone on a spiritual search. He had read many books and seen many different teachers in pursuit of this elusive thing called enlightenment. One day, as he was sitting in his garden at home, suddenly something strange and unexpected happened. All thought, all sense of time, fell away, and all that was left was the absolute freshness and simplicity of this moment. He had a deep realization that the world was somehow perfect as it was, even in its imperfection. The grass, the trees, the wars, the dog poop on the pavement—it was all divine. He knew deeply that everything was in its right place and that he didn't really exist as a separate entity. He was somehow one with all life. He was no longer a person. He was simply an open space of awareness in which life was happening. It felt like his spiritual search had come to an end. He had found the vast, peaceful ocean beyond all the myriad waves. He felt free. He felt as if he would never suffer again.

He remained in this state of deep peace for days. But states and experiences do not last, and soon thoughts and feelings and the complicated story of his life returned. Even though he had experienced a very deep realization of the ocean, the waves began to *hurt* again. He told me how this confused him very much. He had expected that after his "awakening," the waves would stop completely. He had expected the ocean to remain perfectly calm and clear after his realization, and yet these waves—pain waves, sadness waves, fear waves, waves of helplessness and doubt—were still moving in him. And he didn't know what to do with them. He was still experiencing conflict in his relationships. There was much sadness and fear and longing in him that he didn't know how to handle. He was still struggling with his cigarette addiction. How could he be awakened *and* still be suffering? How could he be awakened and still experience doubt and uncertainty and moments of anger? The gurus had promised that awakening would bring the end of all suffering. It didn't make any sense.

During the retreat, we spoke about his post-awakening confusion. We spoke of the deepest acceptance of life, of the inseparability of the waves and the ocean, of the wide-open space that holds everything, of how all waves are allowed in what you are—including all the ones you previously called dark or evil, all the ones that don't fit into your concept of enlightenment. We spoke about the total embrace of life in the present moment—the embrace that you are in your essence—and the discovery of that embrace here and now.

At the end of the retreat, the man told me how he had come to realize that the waves weren't *supposed* to stop. They *were* the ocean. And each wave was a little invitation to see the ocean again, *in* that wave. Even the conflict he was experiencing in his marriage was a giant invitation to wake up and see the ocean *in the midst* of that conflict, to discover which images of himself he was still clinging to, which feelings were not being fully allowed into his experience, how he was shutting himself off from his wife in identifying himself as "the hurt one" when they fought. He had seen the ocean fully, *and* the ocean was still revealing more and more of itself day by day. It was a beautiful paradox.

He then said something beautiful to me: "I used to have this idea that there was something *wrong* with me for not being able to accept the waves and make them go away—like I wasn't strong enough, or awakened enough, or something. But I see now that it's not about me being *strong* enough to accept the waves. The waves of present experience are *already* accepted in what I am. I don't need to accept them. I just notice right now that they are already allowed in. I don't have to be strong enough to accept them. *I'm simply too weak to prevent them from coming in anymore.*"

Enlightenment has nothing to do with being so strong that you are able to accept all the waves. It's not about controlling the waves in any way. It's not about escaping the present moment. It's not about holding up an image of yourself as an enlightened person and proving how spiritual, blissed-out, and peaceful you are all the time. It's about discovering who you are—which is so radically open, so vulnerable, so unprotected, so weak, in a sense, that it becomes more and more impossible for you to escape the waves appearing now. And this weakness isn't really weakness at all, for in this weakness is the greatest strength. It is the deepest acceptance of life. And you don't have to "do" this acceptance—it is how you are built.

Many people have awakening experiences like this man did, in which they touch the vast ocean beyond the multitude of waves. But life doesn't end there. The waves keep coming, and very quickly all of our beautiful spiritual insights are forgotten. No matter how awakened or spiritually evolved we think we are, no matter how much we hold up the image of ourselves as having "no self," or being "nobody," or being "beyond the personal," we get tangled up in the waves of life, whether we admit it or not. We get sucked back into suffering, into physical pain, into relationship conflict, into addictions, into chasing new experiences or holding onto old ones, into more spiritual seeking. It feels as though we were awake, and then we lost that awakening. We touched heaven, and then we fell from it. Great suffering and confusion can result. Once you've touched heaven, life can be hell. Even the most seemingly enlightened person can still suffer sadness or fear or terrible conflict in their relationships after their enlightenment experience. And often they can find this suffering harder than ever to admit, now that they are holding up an image of themselves as "the awakened one," or worse, "the enlightened teacher." But this continued suffering is wonderful news, really, for suffering is just an invitation to let go of all images of yourself, including the image that you're enlightened or that you're beyond suffering; to fearlessly face present experience; and to find the deepest acceptance there—and nowhere else.

Some spiritual teachings talk about stages of awakening. They say that it takes time to become fully awakened. Some teachings say that there can be an initial awakening event (in other words, realizing the ocean), but then it can take many years, even a lifetime, to fully integrate or embody that awakening, to really *live* it in everyday life. Some people talk about awakening as a journey of integrating all the waves, leading to a point in the *future* when all the waves will be fully integrated with the ocean, and they as individuals will be fully, 100-percent-certified awakened. And some people say that there is actually no such thing as awakening at all, that awakening is a myth, that nobody has ever really been awakened, and that we should all just give up on looking at our suffering and have a cup of tea and a cheese sandwich.

There are so many teachings out there, so many different perspectives, and they can all be so confusing for someone who is sincerely interested in finding freedom in their lives. All spiritual paths, processes, practices, and teachings have their place, and I'm not here to judge any one of them. But in recognizing yourself as the wide-open space in which all waves appear and disappear, as the intimate vastness in which all thoughts, sensations, and feelings come and go, it becomes a lot clearer what awakening is really all about.

In recognizing yourself as the vast and intimate open space of awareness, it's no longer a question of something called me becoming *more* awakened over time or reaching total integration in the future, for it is seen that, from the perspective of who I really am, every wave that appears right now is *already* integrated with the ocean—every wave *is* already intimate with what I am. And so it's not a question of me moving toward an end point of total integration in the future. This is the dream of the seeker, who always lives in a story of time and spiritual achievement. It's always, always a question of *recognizing* that integration of present experience *here and now*. It's about awakening to the completeness and deep acceptance of *this* moment, as it is. It's about seeing that *these* waves are already deeply accepted, here and now. Tomorrow's integration is not my job. The story of yesterday's awakening is irrelevant. Here and now is where all life is. And there is *only* here and now.

And although this *seems* to be a process that happens in time—the burning up of false images of yourself, the recognition of seeking in its subtler and subtler forms, the discovery of deep acceptance in those waves you never *imagined* could be accepted, the finding of love and peace in places you thought love and peace had abandoned, the discovery of more and more intimacy in your personal relationship even though you realize deeply that there are no "others" outside of yourself—in fact, it's a timeless process that is only ever happening now. Life integrates itself with itself, here and now, and you are the witness of this dance. Life heals itself through you.

Yes, here is the beautiful paradox of spiritual awakening. Life is already complete, radically complete, here and now. There is nothing wrong with you—even in your imperfection, you are perfect exactly as you are. Life has already completed itself in and as this moment, and this is the beautiful ultimate truth of existence. And yet, equally, that completeness continues to *express* itself as a never-ending invitation to rediscover completeness *in the midst of* this embodied, personal, deeply human experience, here and now.

As each wave appears, as each thought, sound, smell, sensation, feeling arises in the ocean that you are, it gently whispers, "Please, do not turn away from me, however painful or intense I appear right now. Trust me, I am the ocean too. I take this form now. I belong here, although it may not seem obvious. Don't worry, you don't need to accept me; I'm already *in.* And don't worry, you cannot reject me either; I'm already *in.* Have you noticed? Are you willing to go beyond all ideas of yourself, all stories about your past and future, and simply *admit* that I'm already here, that I've already been *admitted?* Can you *admit* that who you really are is vast enough to contain all of life, the good *and* the bad?"

Look at your life. The invitation is everywhere. It is there in the joy and in the pain, in the boredom and in the excitement, in the grief and in the ecstasy, in the sweetness and in the bitterness, at your birth and on your deathbed. The invitation is here, in every single moment of this precious, fragile gift of a life that we so easily take for granted. And right now, even as you read these words, it gently calls you back to itself.

About the Author

Jeff Foster studied astrophysics at Cambridge University. After a long period of depression and illness, in his mid-twenties he became addicted to the idea of spiritual enlightenment and embarked on an intensive spiritual quest for the ultimate truth of existence.

The spiritual search came crashing down with the clear recognition of the nondual nature of everything and the discovery of the extraordinary in the ordinary. In the clarity of this seeing, life became what it always was: intimate, open, loving, and spontaneous, and Jeff was left with a deep understanding of the root illusion behind all human suffering and with a love of the present moment.

He presently holds meetings, retreats, and private one-to-one sessions around the world, gently but directly pointing people back to the deep acceptance inherent in the present moment. He helps people discover who they really are, beyond all spiritual concepts, beyond all thoughts and judgments about themselves, even in the midst of the stress and struggle of modern-day living and intimate relationships. He belongs to no spiritual tradition or lineage and makes his teachings accessible to all.

Jeff was voted number 51 on Watkins Review's 2012 list of the world's "100 Most Spiritually Influential Living People." He lives near Brighton, England. To find out more about Jeff and his teachings, and to view his event schedule, please visit lifewithoutacentre.com.

About Sounds True

Sounds True is a multimedia publisher whose mission is to inspire and support personal transformation and spiritual awakening. Founded in 1985 and located in Boulder, Colorado, we work with many of the leading spiritual teachers, thinkers, healers, and visionary artists of our time. We strive with every title to preserve the essential "living wisdom" of the author or artist. It is our goal to create products that not only provide information to a reader or listener, but that also embody the quality of a wisdom transmission.

For those seeking genuine transformation, Sounds True is your trusted partner. At SoundsTrue.com you will find a wealth of free resources to support your journey, including exclusive weekly audio interviews, free downloads, interactive learning tools, and other special savings on all our titles.

To listen to a podcast interview with Sounds True publisher Tami Simon and author Jeff Foster, please visit SoundsTrue.com/bonus/DeepestAcceptance.